THE BOOK OF
cocktails

THE BOOK OF
cocktails

SALAMANDER

Produced by Salamander Books
An imprint of the Anova Books Company Ltd,
151 Freston Road, London W10 6TH, U.K.

ISBN 1-84065-561-5

1 2 3 4 5 09 08 07 06

Printed in China

All photography © Anova Image Library

Contents

INTRODUCTION

Bar Equipment

You really do not have to be a professional bartender to be able to mix original drinks, providing you use the appropriate tools for the job. You will certainly find some of the utensils listed below already in you home, and you can always improvise with everyday kitchen gadgets. If, however, you go shopping to stock up on bar equipment, the important feature to remember is that the utensils should be easy to clean, which is why stainless-steel items and glass are particularly suitable.

Cocktail shaker

A cocktail shaker is an absolute must for your home bar. It is primarily used to mix drinks with ingredients that are difficult to combine smoothly, such as egg yolks, liqueurs, fruit juices, and cream. Any good bar-supply store will stock a variety of shakers and you are certain to find one to fit your budget and needs. One standard version is a three-part shaker, which consists of a beaker, a lid, and a built-in strainer, to hold back pieces of ice and fruit pits or seeds when pouring the cocktail. Its disadvantage is that the strainer is very difficult to clean and the liquid pours out slowly. The two-part Boston shaker consists of a large stainless-steel beaker and a smaller one made of lead crystal, which fits inside and has the advantage that the glass beaker is also suitable for use as a mixing glass. Professionals usually favor a two-part stainless-steel or silver shaker because it is easier to close than the Boston shaker.

Bar strainer

When you use a two-part shaker or a mixing glass, you will need a round, stainless-steel bar strainer. This features an edge like a coiled spring, and it should fit exactly into the top of the shaker or mixing glass, making it indispensable when straining cocktails so ice and pieces of fruit or pits do not fall into the glass. If necessary, you can use a new tea-strainer instead.

Mixing glass

You will also need a mixing glass, sometimes called a shaker glass, for every drink that is stirred, not shaken, such as clear drinks and those made from easily blended ingredients. When shopping for a mixing glass, look for one with a capacity of about 1 quart (enough for 3 or 4 drinks).

Bar spoon

A long-handled bar spoon is a versatile tool used by bartenders to stir the ingredients in the mixing glass, as a measuring spoon to add the correct amount of ingredients to many cocktails, and to crush flavoring ingredients. Most bar-spoon handles are 10 inches long and made of stainless steel or silver. At the top of the handle there is usually a disc called a muddler used to "muddle," or crush, pieces of fruit, herbs, or sugar cubes. The spoon on the opposite end holds $1/6$ ounce of liquid, or the same amount as a standard kitchen teaspoon. The rounded back of the spoon is also useful for slowly pouring layers of liqueurs into a glass when you do not want the layers to mix. A bar whisk is also useful for stirring and mixing.

Bar measure

A truly indispensable item for your bar is a double-ended bar measure, because exact quantities of ingredients are needed for every drink. Also called a pony-jigger measure, these are usually made of stainless steel with a 1-ounce cup at one end, called a pony, and a $1 1/2$- to 2-ounce measure at the other end, called a jigger. When you go shopping, look for a measure with easy-to-read $1/4$-ounce and $1/2$-ounce markings inside the jigger end. Alternatively, you can use a standard shot glass with markings on it. If you do not have either measure, use a standard set of kitchen measuring spoons—3 teaspoons, or 1 tablespoon, equal $1/2$ ounce, 4 teaspoons equal $3/4$ ounce, and 2 tablespoons equal 1 ounce.

ELECTRIC BLENDER

An electric blender is useful, especially for drinks like frozen daiquiris and those with ingredients that are not easily combined, but it is not essential. To purée fruit, whip cream, or prepare frozen drinks, frappés, and milkshakes, you need a blender with continuous speed adjustment, or you can use an everyday food processor. If drinks with crushed ice become a regular request at your bar or you host many cocktail parties, consider investing in an electric ice shaver.

ICE BUCKET

Use a standard ice bucket, widely available in various sizes and materials, to keep frozen ice cubes conveniently at hand for the duration of any party or cocktail session. Ice tongs or an ice shovel are ideal to remove the ice from the bucket (do not use your fingers), but if you do not have either, use a large spoon.

LEMON JUICER

Fresh fruit juices can be prepared using a lemon squeezer or juicer. Electric juicers are not recommended because they squash the peel and seeds, too.

SIPHON

Many long drinks contain soda water, which is best added to the glass using a siphon. To use one, you simply fill the siphon with water. A carbon dioxide cartridge will make sure the water is always carbonated when you want it.

BAR TONGS

Another very useful tool is a pair of bar tongs, which can be used to loosen tight corks in champagne and other sparkling wines.

DASH BOTTLE

A bitters or dash bottle has a doser cap and is good for storing ingredients that are only used in small dashes.

OTHER EQUIPMENT

The other pieces of equipment that help to make your job behind the bar enjoyable are standard in most kitchens. These include a lemon squeezer and a nutmeg grater. No doubt your kitchen also contains a chopping board (preferably with a drainage channel), a finely serrated knife, similar to a cheese knife, with two points for spearing pieces of fruit, and a citrus zester, also called a cannelle knife, for removing fine strips of citrus peel that make attractive garnishes. Small dishes for holding pieces of fruit and garnishes are also useful, as is a cork with a pouring spout, which can be inserted into any bottle to make pouring out measures easier.

Of course you also need a can opener, a bottle opener, and a corkscrew. A champagne or bottle cooler is indispensable. Toothpicks are an absolute must for spearing olives, cherries, and pearl onions, as well as for creating other garnishes. You might also want to stock up on brightly coloured drinking straws in varying lengths if you plan to serve some of the most exotic cocktails. (Be sure to avoid straws that are too thin, otherwise pieces of ice or fruit can block them.) Different colored and shaped stirrers also make attractive decorations for long drinks.

THE BASICS FOR A SMALL BAR

Here are the "bar essentials" for a complete small bar.
Nothing too fancy. Improvise and tailor your bar to the tastes
of your friends and guests.

BEER, WINE, AND SPIRITS

Beer, lager (refrigerate)
Blended whiskey or rye
Bourbon
Brandy
Gin
Pernod
Red wine, dry French
Rum, light
Scotch
Sherry, dry
Tequila, white
Triple sec
Vermouth, dry and sweet
Vodka (keep in freezer)
White wine, dry French or California
Chardonnay (refrigerate)

MIXERS (KEEP REFRIGERATED, USE FRESH FRUIT JUICES)

Cola
Cranberry juice
Diet soda
Ginger ale
Grapefruit juice
Lemon juice
Lemon-lime soda
Lime juice
Orange juice
Sparkling water
Tomato juice
Tonic water

GARNISHES AND CONDIMENTS

Angostura bitters
Bar sugar
Black pepper
Cocktail olives
Grenadine
Lemons
Limes
Maraschino cherries
Oranges
Tabasco sauce
Worcestershire sauce

GLASSWARE

Brandy snifter
Champagne flute
Cocktail glass
Highball glass
Old-fashioned glass
Pilsner glass
Wine goblet

BARTENDING TOOLS

Bar spoon
Blender
Bottle opener
Citrus reamer
Corkscrew
Jigger
Measuring cup
Measuring spoons
Mixing glass
Paring knife
Standard shaker
Strainer

THE BASICS FOR A FULL HOME BAR

If you have enough room for a full bar, add the following components to those mentioned above. For mixers and ice, you may want to purchase a small refrigerator and keep it next to your liquor cabinet or bar. It is extremely convenient and saves time and space when you are entertaining.

BEER, WINE AND SPIRITS

Aguardiente
Ale (keep in refrigerator)
Amaretto
Amer Picon
Apple brandy
Aquavit
Armagnac
Benedictine
Brut Champagne
Calvados
Campari
Canadian whiskey
Chartreuse, green and yellow
Cognac
Cointreau
Crème de bananes
Crème de cacao, light and dark
Crème de cassis
Crème de menthe, white and green
Crème de noyaux
Curaçao, blue and white
Drambuie
Dubonnet, blanc and rouge
Eau de framboise
Flavored vodkas (citrus, Cherry Heering, pepper, currant; keep in the freezer)
Galliano
Grand Marnier
Grappa
Irish cream liqueur
Irish whiskey
Jagermeister
Kirschwasser
Lillet
Madeira
Maraschino liqueur
Peppermint schnapps

Pernod
Pimm's No. I
Poire
Port (ruby, tawny, and vintage)
Porter
Punt e mes
Rock and rye
Rum, Anejo, dark, Demerara, and gold
Sake
Sherry, fino and cream
Single malt Scotch
Silver tequila
Slivovitz
Sloe gin
Southern Comfort
Stout
Tequila, gold and silver
White Sambuca
Wishniak

MIXERS (KEEP REFRIGERATED)

Apple cider
Beef bouillon
Bitter lemon soda
Clamato juice
Coconut cream
Coffee
Ginger beer
Guava nectar
Half-and-half
Peach nectar
Pineapple juice
Spring water, bottled

GARNISHES AND CONDIMENTS

Allspice
Apples
Bananas
Celery
Cinnamon, ground
Cinnamon sticks
Cocktail onions
Coriander
Cucumber
Eggs *
Honey
Horseradish
Margarita salt
Mint, fresh
Nutmeg, ground
Orange bitters

Orgeat (almond) syrup
Passion fruit syrup
Peaches
Peychaud's Bitters
Pickled jalapeño peppers
Pineapple
Raspberry syrup
Raspberries
Rose's Lime Juice
Semi-sweet chocolate
Strawberries
Sugar cubes
Sugar syrup
Tamarind syrup
White pepper
Whole cloves

* Publisher's note: Please use caution when using raw eggs in any of the recipes included in this book. Raw eggs have been known to cause salmonella poisoning. It is not recommended that pregnant women consume raw eggs.

GLASSWARE

Beer mug
Irish coffee glass
Margarita glass
Pousee café
Punch cup
Red wine glass
Sherry glass
Shot glass
Sour glass
White wine glass

BARTENDING TOOLS

Champagne stopper
Glass pitcher
Ice bucket
Ice tongs
Muddler or mortar and pestle
Punch bowl

MEASUREMENTS

SPIRITS AND WINES

Metric	Imperial	
25 ml.	1 fl. oz.	
50 ml.	2 fl. oz.	
75 ml.	3 fl. oz.	
100 ml.	4 fl. oz.	
150 ml.	5 fl. oz.	($1/4$ pt.)
200 ml.	7 fl. oz.	
250 ml.	8 fl. oz.	(1 cup)
300 ml.	10 fl. oz.	($1/2$ pt.)
350 ml.	12 fl. oz.	
400 ml.	14 fl. oz.	
450 ml.	15 fl. oz.	($3/4$ pt.)
500 ml.	18 fl. oz.	
600 ml.	20 fl. oz.	(1 pt.)
750 ml.	25 fl. oz.	($1 1/4$ pt.)
900 ml.	30 fl. oz.	($1 1/2$ pt.)
1 litre	35 fl. oz.	($1 3/4$ pt.)

BAR MEASUREMENT

Metric	Imperial	
1 dash	$1/32$ fl. oz.	1 ml.
1 teaspoon	$1/8$ fl. oz.	3 ml.
1 tablespoon	$3/8$ fl. oz.	9 ml.
1 pony	1 fl. oz.	25 ml.
1 jigger	$1 1/2$ fl. oz.	38 ml.
1 wine glass	4 fl. oz.	100 ml.
1 split	6 fl. oz.	175 ml.
1 cup	8 fl. oz.	250 ml.

CALORIE COUNTS (APPROXIMATE AMOUNTS)

Alcoholic Beverage	Amount	Calories (KCal)
Beer		
Regular	12 fl. oz.	146
Light	12 fl. oz.	100
Cider, fermented	1 fl. oz.	12

Distilled Spirit	Amount	Calories (Kcal)
Gin, rum, vodka, whiskey		
(80 proof)	1 1/2 fl. oz.	96
(86 proof)	1 1/2 fl. oz.	104
(90 proof)	1 1/2 fl. oz.	109
(94 proof)	1 1/2 fl. oz.	115
(100 proof)	1 1/2 fl. oz.	123

Liqueur	Amount	Calories (KCal)
Brandy, cognac	1 1/2 fl. oz.	75
Coffee liqueur	1 1/2 fl. oz.	176
Crème de menthe	1 1/2 fl. oz.	186
Curaçao	1/2 fl. oz.	60

Wine	Amount	Calories (KCal)
Champagne (sparkling wine)	4 fl. oz.	90
Sherry, dry	2 fl. oz.	84
Table, red	3 1/2 fl. oz.	74
Table, rosé	3 1/2 fl. oz.	73
Table, white	3 1/2 fl. oz.	70
Vermouth, dry	1 fl. oz.	33
Vermouth, sweet	1 fl. oz.	44

Mixers	Amount	Calories (KCal)
Club soda	12 fl. oz.	0
Cola	12 fl. oz.	144
Cranberry juice	3 fl. oz.	54
Diet cola	12 fl. oz.	0
Fresh lemon juice	1 fl. oz.	8
Fresh lime juice	1 fl. oz.	8
Fresh orange juice	2 fl. oz.	28
Ginger ale	12 fl. oz.	124
Heavy cream	1 tbsp.	53
Pineapple juice, unsweetened	2 fl. oz.	34
Tomato juice	2 fl. oz.	12
Tonic water	12 fl. oz.	113

GLASSES

With so many different shapes, sizes and colors in glassware, choosing a suitable glass for a certain drink requires thought. There are classic shapes which suit some cocktails, but nowadays the traditional choice of glass is not that important.

Champagne drinks look attractive when served in a champagne flute and short cocktails may be served in Martini glasses.

Taller drinks need larger glasses and here the choice is more difficult. For tall drinks, with little or no garnish, such as a Bloody Mary or Hummer, a tall highball glass is suitable. Some exotic drinks which are lavishly garnished with slices of fruit, straws, and other decorations need to be served in a substantial glass such as a large goblet. If smaller glasses with narrow necks are heavily garnished, the decoration will interfere with drinking and the effect will not be pleasing.

There are many intriguing glasses available, but beware of overdoing things! Colored glass can spoil the effect of a drink—a dark glass will detract from a delicately pale drink such as a Pink Lady. Heavily patterned glasses can be used, but be sparing with the decoration or the finished result will appear cluttered.

Most important of all, use spotlessly clean glasses. Wash and rinse the glasses in hot water, dry them while still warm and polish with a clean, soft cloth. Check glasses before using and repolish them if necessary.

TYPES OF GLASSES AVAILABLE

Cocktail or Martini glass: a tall, wide-rimmed glass with a tall stem, used for Pink Lady and, of course, Martini.

Brandy snifter: this glass is designed to trap the fragrance of the brandy in the bowl of the glass, so both the aroma and the flavor can be enjoyed.

Wine glass: there are many types of wine glasses so choose a style that is pleasant to drink from. White and red wines can be served in the same style of glass, although traditionally white wine glasses are smaller and have a longer stem.

Liqueur glass: a small glass for serving small measures.

Highball or tall glass: a tall, usually straight sided glass holding about 10–12 fluid oz. Tall drinks mixed with fruit juices or lemonade are best served in highball glasses.

Large goblet: these glasses vary in size and shape. They are used for serving tall mixed drinks with plenty of ice. Exotic drinks, such as Mai Tai or Tropical Cocktail, are best served in goblets. The wide rims allow scope for imaginative decoration without looking cluttered.

Champagne glass: a tall, fluted glass with a tall stem used for champagne cocktails and Ritz Fizz.

Old fashioned or whiskey tumbler: a short tumbler with straight or sloping sides which usually holds about 4–5 fluid oz. Suitable for plain fruit juices, Rusty Nail, and of course, Old Fashioned.

Tulip glass: a tall, tulip shaped glass, often used for champagne drinks.

Garnishes

Citrus Garnishes

Choose firm, colored fruit with unblemished skin. Wash the fruit just before use. A spiral of peel can be used to decorate tall drinks. Pare off about a 2–3 inch strip of peel in a continuous spiral using a canelle knife or vegetable peeler. Take care not to cut into bitter white pith.

Use spiral to hang over rim of the glass into drink.

A knot of peel can be used to add zest to some drinks. Remove strips of peel using a canelle knife or vegetable peeler. Tie each strip into a knot. This releases the fragrant oils from peel. Drop into drink immediately.

A plain slice can be used to decorate drinks. Place orange, lemon, or lime on its side and cut crosswise segments with a sharp, stainless steel knife (a carbon steel knife will discolor flesh).

A decorated slice can be used to garnish a simple drink. Peel may be decorated by scoring skin with a canelle knife or vegetable

peeler. Pull knife round orange, lemon or lime from top to bottom to expose pith. Repeat to make eight divisions.

Place orange, lemon, or lime on its side and cut into thin slices.

Plain and decorated slices can be used in different ways to garnish drinks. Cut through to center of whole, or half slice and place slice on edge of glass. A blood orange can be used to give an attractive effect.

Using a cocktail pick, double up whole slice with cherry in middle. Twist whole or half slices using cocktail pick and balance across rim of glass. A pineapple leaf can be added, if desired.

Twist slices from different colored citrus fruits together.

Cut shapes from fruit peel using a sharp knife or cutter. Float on top of drinks, such as Mulled Wine.

Special cutters can be used to create unusual designs.

A strip of peel can be used to add zest to drinks, such as Martini or Manhattan. Remove thin short strips of zest using a sharp, stainless-steel knife. Longer strips of peel may be used for larger drinks, adding more flavor.

Fruit Garnishes

Strawberry

Choose firm, ripe strawberries with good, green-leaved tops to garnish strawberry flavored drinks and white wine punches.

Cut strawberry in half lengthwise using a stainless-steel knife to prevent discoloration. Use in white wine punches.

Replace green-leaved top of strawberry with sprig of fresh mint. Secure sprig to strawberry using cocktail pick.

Make about a 1-inch cut in to whole strawberry from tip to top, and balance on the glass rim. Cut several times to make a fan.

Kumquat

Kumquats are eaten whole with the peel on. Cut 4 or more sections in the peel with a sharp knife and gently pull each section open to create a kumquat flower. The fruit may also be speared on to a cocktail pick with other fruits, such as pineapple and cherries.

Kiwi fruit

Kiwi fruit adds interesting color to a fruit garnish. Wash fruit and use unpeeled. Cut kiwi fruit into crosswise slices. Make a cut to center of slice and place on edge of glass. Add segments of kiwi fruit to other fruit for decoration. Cut lengthwise and make an upward incision.

Banana

Banana may be used to decorate drinks such as Banana Cow and other exotic cocktails. Choose firm, unblemished fruit with good yellow peel and prepare just before serving.

Cut unpeeled bananas into slices. Dip into lemon juice to avoid discoloration.

Make cut into center of slice and place on rim of glass with a cherry.

PAPAYA OR PAWPAW
Tropical fruit juices are popular mixes for tall drinks and papaya makes an interesting garnish. Choose fruit that is firm but gives slightly with a gentle thumb press. The skin should be unblemished and can vary from green to yellow; use unpeeled. Cut fruit in half lengthwise and remove black seeds.

Cut slices lengthwise to decorate large goblets, making an incision in flesh to help balance on glass.

Cut across papaya and spear small pieces onto cocktail pick with other fruits, such as cherry and slice of starfruit.

Form balls using a melon scoop and spear onto cocktail pick. Add pineapple leaves to decorate.

APPLE
Choose apples with bright red or green skins. Wash before use. Cut apple segments from unpeeled fruit and use to decorate glass. Dip into lemon juice to prevent discoloration.

Cut whole apple in to crosswise slices and float in fruit or wine punches.

STARFRUIT
Choose unblemished yellow or green fruit and wash before use. Cut across fruit to make star-shaped slices and either balance on glass rim or float in drink.

MELON

Melons make an interesting garnish for green or yellow colored drinks, especially those using a melon liqueur. Cut slices of watermelon from a small melon with dark green skin. Make incision in flesh to help balance slice on glass. Add a cherry to decorate.

Use a melon scoop to remove balls from different types of melon for a colorful presentation. Spear melon balls on cocktail pick and serve with short drinks.

COCONUT

To open coconut, pierce "eyes" of coconut with a sharp implement and hammer, then drain out coconut water. Tap coconut with hammer to crack shell and scoop out flesh with a blunt knife. Alternatively, place coconut in a preheated 350F (180C) oven for about 10 minutes and use a hammer to split shell. The flesh will have shrunk away from the skin, allowing easier removal.

Drape coconut segments over edge of glass for exotic drinks. Cut 1/4-inch thick segments from the nut, using a sharp knife and make incision in flesh to help balance coconut on edge of glass. Frost glass with dried coconut mixed with green coloring and add 2 green cherries speared on a cocktail pick.

Use coconut curls to decorate rim of glass. Level edge of coconut with a knife. Pare off

thin peelings of coconut, including brown skin, with a sharp knife, so that they curl up.

Grate coconut flesh on a coarse grater, including brown skin, and sprinkle on top of drinks.

PINEAPPLE

To use the whole pineapple for serving, carefully cut off the top with its spiny leaves, about 2 inches below the leaf growth.

Scoop out the center of the pineapple using a sharp knife and spoon. The flesh may be blended for fresh pineapple juice or used for fruit salad.

Fill the pineapple with the drink, replace top and serve with suitable garnish and straw.

Pineapple leaves can be used as a garnish with other fruits. Remove the best spiny leaves by easing them out gently from the head.

Pineapple slices are used to decorate very large drinks and fruit punches. Lay the pineapple on its side and cut slices approximately $1/2$–$3/4$ inch thick using a stainless-steel knife. Leave on the outside rind as this gives color and texture to the garnish. Cut the slice through to the center, garnish with a cherry and 3 pineapple leaves and place on edge of glass.

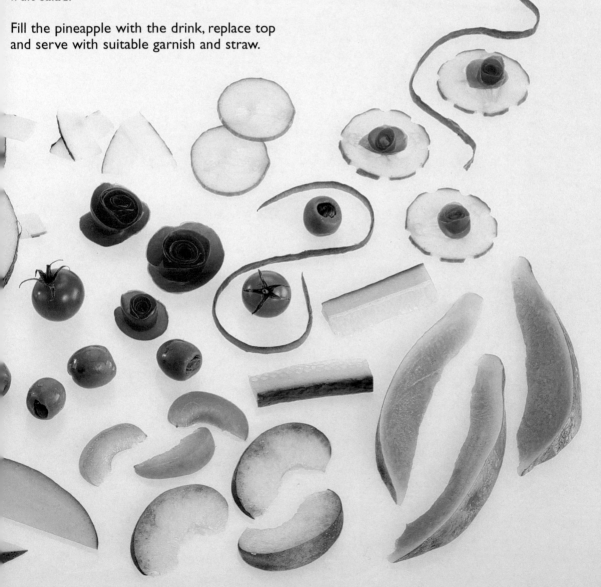

Half slices may be used to garnish cocktails with a tropical flavor. Cut slice in half, make an incision through to center and place on edge of glass. Decorate with 3 pineapple leaves and a cherry.

Quarter slices make an attractive decoration for small glasses. Cut halfway to center and place on edge of glass. Decorate with 2 pineapple leaves and a cherry.

Lengthwise slices can be used to decorate long, tall glasses. Cut a small pineapple in half lengthwise. Cut off a segment and make an incision parallel with the pineapple core. Place on the outside edge of the glass. The top of the pineapple may be left on the segment.

Pineapple pieces can be used to decorate short drinks. Divide a slice of pineapple into 8 equal pieces by cutting diametrically 4 times.

Spear the pieces with a cocktail pick and use for a garnish with colored cherries and pineapple leaves.

CHERRIES
There are many kinds of cocktail cherries available. In addition to the traditional red or green, cherries are colored yellow, blue, purple and orange, and may be flavored with an appropriate liqueur. Spear cherries with a cocktail pick or float on a drink. Choose a color to complement the recipe.

Serve pitted cherries on edge of drink or speared on cocktail pick. A pair of cherries is particularly attractive. Use fresh or cocktail cherries for decoration.

FLOWERS
Rose petals and buds can be used to decorate drinks, such as Ritz Fizz. Choose a tiny, perfect petal or bud and balance it on top of drink.

Delicate orchids are available in sprays from florists. For a special occasion, spear 2 orchids on a cocktail pick and balance on edge of glass. Select the orchid color to complement the drink.

CUCUMBER
Cucumber strips can be used to decorate tall, clear drinks, such as Pimm's. Choose a straight, dark green cucumber and wash and dry before use. Use a canelle knife or vegetable peeler to score along the green skin of the cucumber. Pull the canelle knife towards you, taking off strips of peel.

Cucumber twirls can be hung over the edge of a glass. Peel in a circular movement around the cucumber to produce a twirl.

Decorated cucumber slices can be used to float in clear drinks, or cut to center and balanced on the edge of a glass. Score along length of cucumber with a canelle knife or vegetable peeler, removing 10 to 14 strips of peel. Using a vegetable knife, cut the cucumber into slices.

Cucumber slices make a tasty stirrer for savory drinks, especially those using tomato juice. Cut off the ends of the cucumber. Cut the cucumber in half lengthwise, then slice each half into sticks.

FROSTINGS

SALT

Margarita or Salty Dog can be served in a salt-frosted glass. Hold the glass upside down by its stem to prevent the juice from running down the bowl of the glass and wipe the outside of the glass with a wedge of lemon.

Dip the glass into a dish of salt, until the rim is evenly coated. Celery salt makes an interesting frosting for drinks such as Bloody Mary.

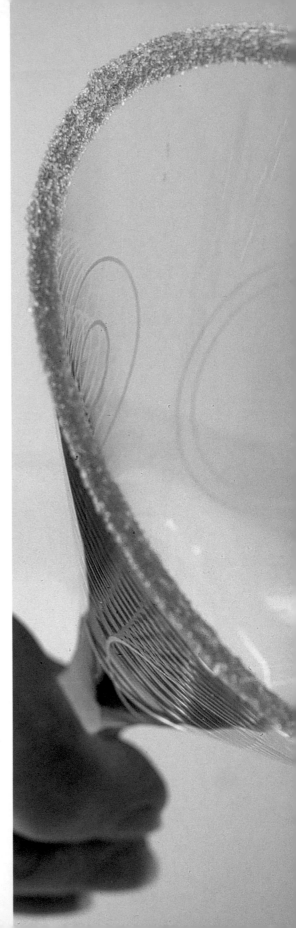

SUGAR

The glass may be wiped with lemon juice, or, for a sweeter frosting, dip the glass in lightly beaten egg white.

Dip the glass into a bowl of sugar. Superfine sugar may be used or, for the more adventurous, try colored or natural brown sugars. Alternatively the glass may be dipped in Grenadine or food coloring and then into a bowl of superfine sugar to give a colored frosting.

COCONUT

For coconut based drinks, dip the glass into a beaten egg white and then into a bowl of dried coconut. Coconut can be tossed with food coloring for a colored frosting.

COFFEE AND CHOCOLATE

For coffee and chocolate liqueur based drinks, wipe the glass with lemon juice or egg white. Dip into instant coffee powder, finely ground coffee beans or unsweetened cocoa powder mixed with a little superfine sugar.

FLAVORFUL TOPPINGS

NUTMEG
Creamy or milky drinks are delicious with a sprinkling of nutmeg. Grate a little of the whole nutmeg onto a plate using a fine grater. Sprinkle carefully onto drink. (Grating directly on to the drink may spoil the finished presentation.) Always grate nutmeg just before serving to prevent loss of flavor.

CINNAMON
Whole sticks of cinnamon may be served with Mulled Wine or Egg Nog to give flavor and to act as a stirrer. Freshly ground cinnamon can be made by grinding the sticks in a coffee grinder. Sprinkle carefully onto drink.

COFFEE
A sprinkling of instant coffee powder may be used on top of coffee-flavored drinks. Alternatively, fresh coffee beans may be finely ground in a coffee or spice grinder.

CHOCOLATE
Chocolate may be grated using a fine or coarse grater and sprinkled over drinks. Chocolate sticks make an interesting garnish for thick, sweet drinks. Twirls of chocolate can be used on top of ice cream and whipped cream. Pull the blade of a sharp knife or vegetable peeler along a block of slightly warm chocolate. The chocolate will curl as it is worked.

ICE

Ice cubes are usually made in oblong ice trays, but experiment with fancy shaped molds for fun. If tap water produces cloudy ice, try using still, spring, or distilled water. For large parties, make up a quantity of ice cubes in advance or buy commercially made ice.

Cracked ice is used in cocktail shakers and chills the drink quickly. Wrap the ice cubes in a clean tea towel and place on a firm surface. Hit the ice with a wooden mallet or rolling pin until the ice has broken into small pieces.

Crushed ice is broken more finely than cracked ice. Ice can be prepared in advance and kept in a plastic bag in the freezing compartment.

Decorated ice cubes can be used in clear drinks. Fill the ice cube tray half full of water and freeze. Dip decoration, such as mint leaves, cherries, slices of orange or lemon segments, kiwi fruit, small kumquats, red currants or slices of stuffed olive in water. Place on the ice cube and freeze until firm.

Top up the ice cubes with cold water and freeze.

Colored and flavored ice cubes can be used to complement the choice of drink. Make ice cubes from cold coffee, tea, ginger ale, or fruit juices, such as orange and apple. One half of the cube may be a different color—simply freeze one layer, such as blackcurrant juice, then freeze the other layer, such as water. Cubes may be flavored, for example, Angostura bitters to use in Pink Gin.

Frozen lemon slices can be used in drinks in place of fresh lemon. Cut lemon into slices and place on a tray in the freezing compartment. Once frozen, lift off, place in a freezer bag, label and tie up.

Serve cocktails in chilled glasses. Place glass in freezer until frosted or swirl an ice cube around the glass for a few minutes to achieve the same effect. Do not place very fragile glasses in freezer, as they may crack in the extreme temperature. Remove ice cubes before adding drink.

HOW TO MIX COCKTAILS

PREPARING DRINKS IN A SHAKER

This is how cocktails containing ingredients that are difficult to combine—such as eggs, milk, liqueurs, and syrups—are prepared. Fill the cocktail shaker up to two-thirds full with ice cubes and swirl them round briefly. Put the shaker or glass liner in the refrigerator to chill.

Strain any water from the melting ice cubes out of the shaker. Measure out the ingredients according to the recipe, add them to the shaker, and close it tightly. Shake the shaker firmly for a few seconds, moving it in and out from the body. Drinks that are easy to mix should be shaken for about 10 seconds, while drinks using egg yolk need about 20 seconds.

Open the shaker and strain the drink through the bar sieve into a chilled glass. Garnish the drink, if desired. A perfectly shaken cocktail looks cloudy at first, then slowly clears from bottom to top. Ingredients for no more than two cocktails should be shaken together in a Boston shaker (if extra cocktails are required, use more ice).

PREPARING DRINKS IN A BLENDER

You usually use a blender for mixing drinks that contain cream, eggs, fruit, and ice, as well as for those that are frozen. First chill a suitable glass in the refrigerator. If the drink has an elaborate garnish, assemble it now so the drink can be served as soon as it is blended. Put 1 scoop of crushed ice or 2 or 3 ice cubes into the blender jug.

Measure out the ingredients according to the recipe and put them into the blender jug. Make sure the lid is properly closed. Now run the blender for about 10 seconds on the first setting then switch to the second setting

and blend for 10 seconds longer. If the drink is too thick, add some more crushed ice or ice cubes to the blender jug before switching the blender to setting 2.

Pour the drink into the prepared glass, garnish, and serve immediately.

PREPARATION IN A MIXING GLASS

All drinks that are stirred together with ice cubes, but which are served without ice, are prepared in a mixing glass. First chill a suitable glass. If the drink has an elaborate garnish, assemble it now so the drink can be served as soon as it is mixed. Put 2 or 3 ice cubes in the mixing glass and swirl them around a few times.

Strain the melted ice water out of the mixing glass. Now mix everything together, working from bottom to top, with a long-handled bar spoon.

Strain the drink immediately through the bar sieve into the chilled glass and garnish if desired. If cocktails for several people are being mixed (remember to add more ice), it is better to pour less into the glasses initially, and then share out the rest equally.

PREPARATION IN THE GLASS

Generally, drinks whose ingredients combine easily are stirred in the glass in which they will be served. First chill a suitable glass. If the drink has an elaborate garnish, assemble it now so the drink can be served as soon as it is blended. Put 2 or 3 ice cubes into the chilled glass.

Measure out the ingredients according to the recipe and add them to the glass.

Carefully stir the drink with a bar spoon, garnish if desired, and serve immediately.

FLAVORING WITH LEMON OR ORANGE PEEL

Many cocktails are flavored in the glass with the zest from a piece of lemon or orange peel. To do this, pare a small, round piece of peel (without any bitter white pith) from an unwaxed, organic citrus fruit. With the peel facing downward, take the piece of peel between your fingers and squeeze. The essential oils from the peel will squirt into the drink, adding an extra twist of flavor.

PROFESSIONAL TIPS AND HINTS

As a novice drinks mixer you should follow the quantities specified in the recipes exactly.

Frequently used quantities in the recipes are:

- 1 dash = The amount that flows out of the dash bottle through the pourer when it is inverted once.
- 1 shot = 2 teaspoons
- 1 tsp. or 1 bar spoon = $1/6$ ounce
- 1 tbsp. = $1/2$ ounce

For recipes that are prepared for several people (such as bowls and punches), quantities are also given in cups and quarts. When a bottle of wine or liquor is specified, it is a standard 750-ml. bottle.

Unless otherwise specified, the recipes are intended for 1 glass (1 person).

When mixing drinks, cleanliness is paramount. Wash all equipment, such as the shaker, mixing glass, bar strainer, and bar spoon, thoroughly and immediately after use. Also, use ice tongs, a fork or spoon to put ice cubes or pieces of fruit into glasses, not your fingers.

If you want to serve drinks in chilled glasses, you have two options. Either put the glasses in the freezer until they are frosted with a film of ice, or chill them with ice cubes. If you are going to use the freezer, however, only use a freezerproof glass.

Cocktails that are served with complicated garnishes, such as fruit kabobs or citrus peel, are best served on a small plate or cocktail napkin. This gives the drinker somewhere to put the garnish when it is removed from the glass.

According to international conventions, a drink should not contain more than 2 ounces alcohol and no more than five ingredients. The total volume of a long drink should not exceed 9 ounces.

Champagne and sparkling wines, juices, carbonated beverages, and mineral water should always be kept in a refrigerator.

Carbonated ingredients, such as soft drinks, soda water, and sparkling wine, should never be shaken in the cocktail shaker.

Only use unwaxed, citrus fruits for garnishes, squeezing and adding to drinks (even in bowls and punches). These should be washed thoroughly before use, as should all other varieties of fruit.

When serving long drinks, place a straw and stirrer in the glass.

Drinks that should be shaken can also be prepared using an electric blender.

For the sake of simplicity, a cocktail glass is always suggested in the recipes. It is, however, up to you whether you use a cocktail glass or a wide-mouth champagne glass.

The recipes for bowls, punches, and mulled wines include ingredients that are given in bottles. These are standard 750-ml. bottles.

Some drinks are first prepared with ice cubes and then strained (without ice cubes) into a glass that contains fresh ice cubes. In this way, the drink is not diluted so quickly and remains well chilled. In the recipes, the rule is always to strain the drink into a glass with ice cubes.

RUM-BASED DRINKS

RUM

RUM GIMLET

FRUITY, FRESH DRINK FOR HOT DAYS

- Rocks glass
- 1 1/2 ounces dark rum
- 3/4 ounce lime cordial
- Extra: 1 lime quarter

Mix the ingredients together, with ice cubes, in the glass. Squeeze the juice from the lime quarter over the drink and add the crushed lime to the glass.

RUM ALEXANDER

SWEET AFTER-DINNER DRINK

- Cocktail glass
- Shaker
- 3/4 ounce dark rum
- 3/4 ounce brown crème de cacao
- 3/4 ounce light cream
- Extra: Grated nutmeg

Shake all the ingredients together, with ice cubes, in the shaker and strain into the cocktail glass. Sprinkle a little nutmeg on top of the drink.

DAVIS

ALCOHOLIC DRINK FOR A PARTY

- Cocktail glass
- Shaker
- 3/4 ounce dark rum
- 3/4 ounce dry vermouth
- 2 tsp. grenadine
- 2 tsp. lemon juice

Shake all the ingredients together, with ice, in the shaker and strain into the cocktail glass.

UPTON

FRUITY APERITIF OR AFTER-DINNER DRINK

- Cocktail glass
- Shaker
- 3/4 ounce dark rum
- 3/4 ounce pineapple juice
- 2 tsp. orange juice
- 2 tsp. lemon juice

Shake all the ingredients together, with ice, in the shaker and strain into the cocktail glass.

CALCUTTA FLIP

CREAMY, SWEET DRINK FOR THE EVENING

- Champagne flute or flip glass
- Shaker
- 1 1/2 ounces dark rum
- 1 1/2 ounces light cream
- 3/4 ounce sugar syrup
- 2 tsp. orange-flavored liqueur
- 1 egg yolk
- Extra: Grated nutmeg

Shake all the ingredients together, with ice, in the shaker and strain into the glass. Sprinkle a little grated nutmeg on top of the drink.

RUM STINGER

SPICY DRINK FOR THE EVENING

- Cocktail glass
- Mixing glass
- 1 1/2 ounces dark rum
- 3/4 ounce white crème de menthe

Mix the ingredients together, with ice, in the mixing glass and strain into the glass.

RUM

MAI TAI

FRUITY, MILD DRINK FOR A PARTY

- Large goblet
- Crushed ice
- 2 ounces light rum
- 1 ounce dark rum
- 1/2 ounce curaçao or other orange-flavored liqueur
- 1/2 ounce Orgeat or other almond-flavored syrup
- 1/2 ounce lemon or lime juice

GARNISH
- Slice of pineapple
- 1 maraschino cherry
- Slice of orange

Half-fill large goblet with ice. Mix in light rum, dark rum, curaçao, Orgeat, and lemon or lime juice. Fill glass with more crushed ice and stir contents gently. Spear fruit with a toothpick and rest on top of glass.

OCHO RIOS

FRUITY, SWEET DRINK FOR A PARTY

- Large cocktail glass
- Shaker
- 1 1/2 ounces dark rum
- 1 1/2 ounces guava nectar
- 3/4 ounce sugar syrup
- 3/4 ounce lime cordial
- 3/4 ounce light cream

Shake all the ingredients together in the shaker and strain into the cocktail glass.

RUM TONIC

TANGY, DRY DRINK FOR A PARTY

- Highball/Collins glass
- 1 1/2 ounces dark rum
- Tonic water for topping up
- Extra: 1 lime quarter

Pour the rum into the highball glass with some ice cubes. Top up with tonic water and stir briefly. Squeeze the juice from the lime quarter over the drink and add the crushed lime to the glass.

Mai Tai

RUM

PARISIAN BLONDE

MEDIUM-DRY AFTER-DINNER DRINK

- Cocktail glass
- Shaker
- 3/4 ounce dark rum
- 3/4 ounce triple sec
- 3/4 ounce light cream

Shake all the ingredients together, with ice, in the shaker and strain into the glass.

RUM COLLINS

REFRESHING COLLINS FOR ANY TIME OF DAY

- Collins/highball glass
- 1 1/2 ounces dark rum
- 3/4 ounce lemon juice
- 2 tsp. sugar syrup
- Soda water for topping up

GARNISH
- 1/2 slice of lemon
- 1 maraschino cherry

Mix the rum, lemon juice, and sugar syrup together, with ice, in the highball glass. Top up with soda water and stir. Perch the fruit on the rim of the glass.

FINN DINGHY

MEDIUM-DRY DRINK FOR ANY OCCASION

- Highball/Collins glass
- Shaker
- 2 ounces pineapple juice
- 3/4 ounce dark rum
- 3/4 ounce Malibu or other coconut-flavored liqueur
- 2 tsp. passion-fruit syrup
- 1 dash lemon juice

GARNISH
1/2 slice of orange
2 maraschino cherries

Shake all the ingredients together, with ice, in the shaker and strain into the highball glass over crushed ice. Spear the slice of orange and cherries on a long toothpick so they look like a sail and put the garnish into the glass.

HEARTBREAKER

- Highball/Collins glass
- Shaker
- 2 ounces orange juice
- 2 ounces pineapple juice
- 1 ounce dark rum
- 3/4 ounce cherry brandy

GARNISH
- 1/4 slice of pineapple
- 1 maraschino cherry

REFRESHING DRINK FOR A PARTY

Shake the ingredients together, with ice, in the shaker and strain into the Collins glass over the ice cubes. Perch the fruit on the rim of the glass.

BARBADOS

- Highball/Collins glass
- Shaker
- 2 3/4 ounces orange juice
- 1 1/2 ounces dark rum
- 2 tsp. grenadine
- 2 tsp. lemon juice
- 1 dash orange bitters

GARNISH
- 1/4 slice of pineapple
- Sprig of mint

FRUITY DRINK FOR THE EVENING

Shake all the ingredients together, with ice, in the shaker and strain into the highball glass over ice cubes. Spear the slice of pineapple and sprig of mint on a toothpick and perch the pineapple on the rim of the glass.

EASTWARD

- Highball/Collins glass
- Shaker
- 1 1/2 ounces cream of coconut
- 1 1/2 ounces pineapple juice
- 1 ounce dark rum
- 3/4 ounce amaretto
- 2 tsp. lime cordial

GARNISH
- 1/4 slice of pineapple
- 1 maraschino cherry
- Sprig of mint

FRUITY, SWEET DRINK FOR EVERY DAY

Shake the ingredients together, with ice, in the shaker and strain into the highball glass over ice cubes. Perch the slice of pineapple on the rim of the glass and fasten the cherry to it with a small toothpick. Put the sprig of mint into the glass.

RUM

COLUMBUS

REFRESHING DRINK FOR HOT DAYS

- Highball/Collins glass
- 1 ounce dark rum
- 2 tsp. apricot-flavored liqueur
- 2 tsp. grenadine
- Bitter lemon for topping up

GARNISH
- 1/2 slice lemon

Pour the ingredients into the highball glass, with ice cubes, and stir well. Perch the slice of lemon on the rim of the glass. Serve with a long stirrer.

RUM EGGNOG

FILLING AFTER-DINNER DRINK

- Large rocks glass
- Shaker
- 3 1/2 ounces milk or light cream
- 1 1/2 ounces dark rum
- 2 tsp. sugar syrup
- 1 egg yolk
- Extra: Grated nutmeg

Shake the ingredients together firmly, with ice, in the shaker and strain into the glass. Sprinkle a little grated nutmeg on top.

TAHITI

FRUITY DRINK FOR A PARTY

- Highball/Collins glass
- Shaker
- 2 3/4 ounces orange juice
- 1 ounce dark rum
- 1 ounce Malibu or other coconut-flavored liqueur
- 3/4 ounce lemon juice

GARNISH
- 3 strips of coconut

Shake all the ingredients together, with ice, in the shaker and pour into the glass. Perch the strips of coconut on the rim of the glass.

FEDORA PUNCH

SLIGHTLY BITTER DRINK FOR A PARTY

- Highball/Collins glass
- Shaker
- 1 ounce dark rum
- 3/4 ounce lemon juice
- 3/4 ounce sugar syrup
- 2 tsp. cognac
- 2 tsp. bourbon
- 2 tsp. orange curaçao

GARNISH
1 lemon peel spiral

Shake all the ingredients together in the shaker and strain into the glass, half filled with crushed ice. Perch the spiral of peel on the rim of the glass.

HAWAIIAN BANGER

SPICY, MILD DRINK FOR A PARTY

- Highball/Collins glass
- 2 3/4 ounces orange juice
- 1 1/2 ounces dark rum
- 3/4 ounce Galliano

GARNISH
- 1/2 slice of orange
- 1 maraschino cherry

Mix all the ingredients together, with ice cubes, in the highball glass. Spear the slice of orange and the cherry on a toothpick and put it in the drink. Serve with a straw.

MAGIC QUEEN

FRUITY DRINK FOR HOT DAYS

- Highball/Collins glass
- Shaker
- 1 1/2 ounces dark rum
- 1 ounce orange juice
- 3/4 ounce pineapple juice
- 2 tsp. triple sec
- 2 tsp. banana-flavored liqueur
- 2 tsp. lemon juice
- 1 tsp. grenadine

GARNISH
- 1/2 slice of lemon
- 1/2 slice of orange
- 1 maraschino cherry

Shake the ingredients together, with ice, in the shaker and strain into the highball glass over crushed ice. Spear the fruit on a toothpick and lay the garnish across the rim of the glass.

RUM

ZOMBIE

FRUITY DRINK FOR A SUMMER PARTY

- Highball/Collins glass
- Shaker
- 1 3/4 ounces pineapple juice
- 3/4 ounce light rum
- 3/4 ounce dark rum
- 3/4 ounce lemon or lime juice
- 2 tsp. apricot brandy
- 3/4 ounce rum (150 proof)

GARNISH
- 1 slice of orange
- 1 maraschino cherry
- Sprig of mint

Shake all the ingredients, except the 150-proof rum, together, with ice, in the shaker and strain into the highball glass over crushed ice. Spear the slice of orange and cherry on a toothpick, lay the garnish across the rim of the glass, and add the sprig of mint to the glass. Pour the 150-proof rum into the glass. Serve with a stirrer and straw.

EL PRESIDENTE

FRUITY APERITIF

- Cocktail glass
- Shaker
- 1 ounce dark rum
- 3/4 ounce orange juice
- 2 tsp. dry vermouth
- 1 dash grenadine
- 1 dash orange curaçao

Shake all the ingredients together firmly, with ice, in the shaker and strain into the glass.

JAMAICA KISS

CREAMY AFTER-DINNER DRINK

- Cocktail glass
- 3/4 ounce dark rum
- 3/4 ounce crème de café
- 3/4 ounce light cream

Pour the rum and crème de café into the cocktail glass. Float the cream on top of the drink.

Zombie

RUM

ELISA

MEDIUM-DRY AFTER-DINNER DRINK

- Cocktail glass
- Mixing glass
- I ounce dark rum
- 2 tsp. Amaro Averna bitters
- 2 tsp. apricot brandy
- 2 tsp. sweet white vermouth
- 2 tsp. dry champagne or sparkling wine

GARNISH
- I piece of orange peel
- I maraschino cherry

Mix all the ingredients, except the champagne, together, with ice, in the mixing glass and strain into the glass. Top up with champagne. Spear the orange peel and cherry on a toothpick and lay the garnish across the rim of the glass.

MALLORCA

MEDIUM-DRY AFTER-DINNER DRINK

- Cocktail glass
- Mixing glass
- I ounce dark rum
- 2 tsp. dry vermouth
- 2 tsp. crème de banane
- 2 tsp. Drambuie

Mix the ingredients together, with ice, in the mixing glass and strain into the glass.

ANDALUSIA

DRY AFTER-DINNER DRINK

- Cocktail glass
- Mixing glass
- 2 ounces dry sherry
- I ounce brandy
- I ounce light rum
- 1/4 tsp. Angostura bitters

Mix the ingredients together, with ice in a mixing glass. Stir and strain into a cocktail glass.

Rum Kum

FRUITY, MILD DRINK FOR A PARTY

- Large cocktail glass
- Mixing glass
- 1 1/2 ounces dark rum
- 1 ounce lime cordial
- 3/4 ounce orange curaçao

GARNISH
- 1 kumquat

Mix all the ingredients together in the mixing glass and strain into the cocktail glass. Perch the kumquat on the rim of the glass.

Carib

FRUITY, SPICY DRINK FOR A PARTY

- Cocktail glass
- Shaker
- 1 ounce dark rum
- 1 ounce gin
- 3/4 ounce lemon juice
- 2 tsp. sugar syrup

GARNISH
- 2 maraschino cherries

Shake all the ingredients together, with ice, in the shaker and strain into the cocktail glass. Spear the cherries on a toothpick and lay across the rim of the glass.

Trophy

FRUITY, BITTER DRINK FOR THE EVENING

- Cocktail glass
- Shaker
- 2 ounces dark rum
- 3/4 ounce lime juice
- 1 tsp. confectioners' sugar
- 3 dashes Angostura bitters

Shake all the ingredients together in the shaker and strain into the glass.

RUM

TRINIDAD PUNCH

- Large goblet
- Shaker
- 3 ounces rum
- 2 ounces lime juice
- 1 tsp. sugar syrup
- 2–3 dashes Angostura bitters
- Ice cubes

GARNISH
- Lemon peel
- Grated nutmeg

DELICIOUS, BITTER COCKTAIL FOR THE EVENING

Shake all the ingredients together in the shaker with a scoop of ice. Cover and shake vertically until the shaker is frosty. Strain into the glass half-filled with ice cubes. Garnish with lemon peel and dust with nutmeg.

PUERTO PUNCH

- Highball/Collins glass
- Shaker
- 1 1/2 ounces orange juice
- 1 1/2 ounces pineapple juice
- 3/4 ounce dark rum
- 3/4 ounce Southern comfort
- 2 tsp. lemon juice

GARNISH
- 1/2 slice orange
- 1 maraschino cherry

FRUITY, REFRESHING DRINK FOR A SUMMER PARTY

Shake the ingredients together, with ice, in the shaker and strain into the highball glass over crushed ice. Perch the slice of orange on the rim of the glass and fasten the cherry to it with a toothpick.

PLANTER'S COCKTAIL

- Rocks glass
- Shaker
- 1 3/4 ounces dark rum
- 1 ounce orange juice
- 3/4 ounce lemon juice

GARNISH
- 1/2 slice of lemon
- 1/2 slice of orange

FRUITY, TANGY DRINK FOR HOT DAYS

Shake all the ingredients together, with ice, in the shaker and pour into the glass over crushed ice. Perch the slices of fruit on the rim of the glass.

Trinidad Punch

RUM

BOSSA NOVA

FRUITY, MILD DRINK FOR A SUMMER PARTY

- Highball/Collins glass
- Shaker
- 2 ounces pineapple juice
- 1 ounce dark rum
- 3/4 ounce Galliano
- 2 tsp. apricot brandy

GARNISH
- 1 slice of orange
- 1/4 apricot

Shake all the ingredients together, with ice, in the shaker and pour into the glass. Perch the fruit on the rim of the glass.

CHERRY DAIQUIRI

TANGY, SHORT APERITIF

- Cocktail glass
- Mixing glass
- 1 ounce light rum
- 3/4 ounce cherry brandy
- 3/4 ounce lime cordial
- 2 tsp. kirsch

GARNISH
- 1 maraschino cherry

Mix all the ingredients together, with ice, in the mixing glass and strain into the glass. Add the cherry to the glass.

PINK RUM

FRUITY, MILD LONG DRINK FOR EVERY DAY

- Highball/Collins glass
- 1 1/2 ounces dark rum
- 3/4 ounce lime juice
- 3/4 ounce grenadine
- Bitter lemon for topping up
- Extra: 1/4 lime

Mix together the rum, lime juice, and grenadine, with ice, in the highball glass. Top up with bitter lemon and stir briefly. Squeeze the juice from the lime quarter into the drink. Add the crushed lime quarter to the glass. Serve with a straw.

MOJITO

- Highball/Collins glass
- A few mint leaves
- 3/4 ounce lemon or lime juice
- 2 tsp. sugar syrup
- 1 1/2 ounces light rum
- Soda water for topping up

GARNISH
- Sprig of mint

REFRESHING DRINK FOR A SUMMER PARTY

Put the mint leaves in the glass and crush them. Add the lemon, or lime juice, and sugar syrup and stir. Add plenty of crushed ice and the rum; stir again. Top up with soda water. Put the sprig of mint into the glass.

CORAL SEA

- Highball/Collins glass
- Shaker
- 1 3/4 ounces cream of coconut
- 1 3/4 ounces pineapple juice
- 1 ounce light rum
- 3/4 ounce blue curaçao
- 2 tsp. light cream

GARNISH
- 1/4 slice of pineapple
- 1 maraschino cherry
- 1 mint leaf

CREAMY, SWEET DRINK FOR A PARTY

Shake all the ingredients together, with ice, in the shaker and strain into the highball glass over crushed ice. Spear the fruit and mint leaf on a toothpick, and lay the garnish across the rim of the glass.

MONTEGO BAY

- Highball/Collins glass
- Shaker
- 1 1/2 ounces light rum
- 3/4 ounce lemon juice
- 3/4 ounce lime cordial
- 2 tsp. blue curaçao
- Extra: 1 lime quarter

FRUITY, SWEET-AND-SOUR DRINK FOR A SUMMER PARTY

Shake all the ingredients together, with ice, in the shaker and strain into the glass, half-filled with crushed ice. Add the lime quarter. Serve with a straw.

ICED PEACH DAIQUIRI

- Highball/Collins glass
- Blender
- 1 ripe peach
- 1 1/4 ounces white rum
- 3/4 ounce peach brandy
- Juice of 1/2 lime
- 1 tsp. sugar syrup

GARNISH
- 1 lime peel spiral
- 1 maraschino cherry

FRUITY, SUMMER DRINK

Remove skin from peach and put the flesh in the blender. Add the rest of the ingredients and blend until it is slushy. Pour unstrained into the glass and garnish with the fruit.

JAMAICA GREEN

- Highball/Collins glass
- Shaker
- 1 1/2 ounces light rum
- 1 ounce lemon juice
- 3/4 ounce green crème de menthe
- 3/4 ounce sugar syrup

GARNISH
- 1 slice of lemon

DELICATE, TANGY DRINK FOR A SUMMER PARTY

Shake all the ingredients together, with ice, in the shaker and pour into the highball glass. Perch the slice of lemon on the rim of the glass.

MAHUKONA

- Highball/Collins glass
- 1 1/2 ounces of light rum
- 1 ounce lemon juice
- 3/4 ounce triple sec
- 3/4 ounce sugar syrup
- 1 dash Angostura bitters
- Extra: 1 slice of diced pineapple, 3 maraschino cherries

FRUITY, SWEET-AND-SOUR DRINK FOR A PARTY

Mix all the ingredients together, with ice cubes, in the highball glass. Add the fruit to the glass. Serve with a straw and a long-handled spoon.

Iced Peach Daiquiri

RUM

Hula Hula

FRUITY, MILD DRINK FOR A SUMMER PARTY

- Balloon-shaped wine glass
- Shaker
- 1 3/4 ounces passion-fruit juice
- 1 ounce dark rum
- 1 ounce light rum
- 1 ounce sugar syrup
- 1 ounce lemon juice

GARNISH
- 1 slice of kiwi fruit
- 1 slice of star fruit

Shake all the ingredients together, with ice, in the shaker and pour into the glass. Perch the fruit on the rim of the glass. Serve with a straw.

Bahia

FRUITY, SWEET DRINK FOR HOT DAYS

- Highball/Collins glass
- Shaker
- 1 1/2 ounces mango juice
- 1 ounce dark rum
- 1 ounce light rum
- 1 ounce cream of coconut

GARNISH
- 1 slice of orange
- 1 slice of star fruit
- 1 maraschino cherry

Shake all the ingredients together, with ice, in the shaker and pour into the highball glass. Perch the fruit on the rim of the glass.

Barbados Swizzle

FRUITY, TANGY DRINK FOR THE SUMMER

- Highball/Collins glass
- 1 3/4 ounces light rum
- 3/4 ounce lime juice
- 2 tsp. sugar syrup
- 1 dash Angostura bitters

GARNISH
- Sprig of mint
- 1 lime peel spiral

Pour all the ingredients together into the highball glass, top up with the crushed ice, and stir. Add the sprig of mint to the glass and hang the spiral of lime peel over the rim of the glass.

RUM COOLER

TANGY, REFRESHING LONG DRINK FOR THE EVENING

- Highball/Collins glass
- Shaker
- 2 ounces lime juice
- 1 1/2 ounces light rum
- 1/2 ounce Galliano

GARNISH
- 1 slice of lime
- 1 maraschino cherry

Shake the ingredients together, with ice, in the shaker and strain into the highball glass over crushed ice. Spear the fruit on a toothpick and lay the garnish across the rim of the glass.

SWIMMING POOL

SWEET, FRUITY DRINK FOR A SUMMER PARTY

- Highball/Collins glass
- Shaker
- 1 3/4 ounces cream of coconut
- 1 3/4 ounces pineapple juice
- 1 ounce light rum
- 3/4 ounce vodka
- 2 tsp. light cream
- 2 tsp. blue curaçao

GARNISH
- 1/4 slice of pineapple
- 1 maraschino cherry

Shake all the ingredients, except the blue curaçao, together firmly, with ice, in the shaker and strain into the highball glass over the crushed ice. Pour the curaçao into the drink. Spear the piece of pineapple and maraschino cherry on a toothpick and lay the garnish across the rim of the glass.

RUM SOUR

REFRESHING SOUR FOR THE SUMMER

- Sour glass or rocks glass
- Shaker
- 1 3/4 ounces light or dark rum
- 3/4 ounce sugar syrup
- 3/4 ounce lemon juice
- 1 shot soda water (optional)

GARNISH
- 1 slice of lemon
- 1 maraschino cherry

Shake the rum, lemon juice, and sugar syrup together, with ice, in the shaker and strain into the glass. Add a shot of soda water and stir briefly. Perch the fruit on the rim of the glass.

Coconut Daiquiri

- Large goblet
- Shaker
- 1 ounce light rum
- 2 ounces coconut liqueur
- 4 ounces of lime juice
- Dash of egg white

Fruity, mild drink

Mix the ingredients in the shaker with a scoop of ice. Cover and shake until the shaker is frosty. Strain into a goblet.

Bacardi Cooler

- Highball/Collins glass
- Shaker
- 1 1/2 ounces Bacardi or light rum
- 3/4 ounce lemon juice
- 2 tsp. grenadine
- Tonic water for topping up
Garnish
- 1 lemon peel spiral

Refreshing, bitter cooler for a summer party

Shake all the ingredients, except the tonic water, together, with ice, in the shaker and pour into the highball glass. Top up with tonic water. Add the lemon peel spiral to the glass. Serve with a stirrer.

Don Frederico

- Highball/Collins glass
- Shaker
- 1 ounce light rum
- 1/2 ounce Galliano
- 1/2 ounce grenadine
- 2 dashes apricot brandy
- Orange juice for topping up
Garnish
- 1 piece of orange peel

Fruity, refreshing long drink for a party

Shake all the ingredients, except the orange juice, together, with ice, in the shaker and strain into the highball glass. Top up with the orange juice and stir, then perch the orange peel on the rim of the glass.

Coconut Daiquiri

RUM

TROPICAL WONDER

FRUITY, MILD DRINK FOR ANY TIME OF THE YEAR

- Highball/Collins glass
- Shaker
- 1 1/2 ounces light rum
- 1 1/2 ounces passion-fruit juice
- 1 1/2 ounces orange juice
- 1 1/2 ounces pineapple juice

GARNISH
- 1 slice of orange
- 1 slice of lime
- 1 sprig of lemon balm

Shake all the ingredients together, with ice, in the shaker and strain into the glass. Perch the fruit and sprig of lemon balm on the rim of the glass.

FIREMAN'S SOUR

REFRESHING DRINK FOR HOT DAYS

- Highball/Collins glass
- Shaker
- 3/4 ounce light rum
- 3/4 ounce lemon juice
- 2 tsp. grenadine
- Soda water for topping up

GARNISH
- 1/2 slice of orange
- 1 maraschino cherry

Shake all the ingredients, except the soda water, together, with plenty of ice, in the shaker. Pour into the glass and top up with soda water. Spear the slice of orange and cherry on a toothpick, and lay the garnish across the rim of the glass.

PEDRO COLLINS

REFRESHING DRINK FOR ANY TIME OF THE DAY

- Collins/highball glass
- 1 1/2 ounces light rum
- 3/4 ounce lemon juice
- 2 tsp. sugar syrup
- Soda water for topping up

GARNISH
- 1/2 slice of lemon
- 1 maraschino cherry

Mix the rum, lemon juice, and sugar syrup together, with ice, in the Collins glass. Top up with the soda water and stir. Spear the fruit on a toothpick and lay the garnish across the rim of the glass.

BALI DREAM

FRUITY DRINK FOR THE EVENING

- Highball/Collins glass
- Shaker
- 2³/4 ounces pineapple juice
- 1 ounce light rum
- 1 ounce Pisang Ambon
- ³/4 ounce cream of coconut

GARNISH
- ¹/4 slice of pineapple
- 1 maraschino cherry

Shake all the ingredients together firmly, with ice, in the shaker and strain into the highball glass over crushed ice. Perch the slice of pineapple over the rim of the glass and fasten the cherry to it with a toothpick.

BANANA DAIQUIRI

FRUITY DRINK FOR A SUMMER PARTY

- Champagne or cocktail glass
- Shaker
- 1 ounce light or dark rum
- 1 ounce lemon juice
- ³/4 ounce banana-flavored liqueur
- 2 tsp. sugar syrup

GARNISH
- 1 slice of banana

Shake all the ingredients together, with ice cubes, in the shaker and strain into the glass. Perch the slice of banana on the rim of the glass.

LASER

FRUITY, MEDIUM-DRY DRINK FOR ANY OCCASION

- Highball/Collins glass
- Shaker
- 2 ounces passion-fruit juice
- 1 ounce light rum
- ³/4 ounce Southern Comfort
- ³/4 ounce lemon juice
- 2 tsp. mandarin syrup

GARNISH
- ¹/2 slice of orange
- 2 maraschino cherries

Shake all the ingredients together firmly, with ice, in the shaker and strain into the highball glass over crushed ice. Spear the cherries and slice of orange on a long toothpick so they form the shape of a sail and put the garnish in the glass. Serve with a stirrer.

RUM

BLUE HAWAIIAN

- Large goblet
- Shaker
- 2 ounces pineapple juice
- 1 ounce light rum
- 1 ounce blue curaçao
- 1 ounce coconut cream

GARNISH
- 1 slice of pineapple
- Strip of coconut

CREAMY, SWEET DRINK FOR A PARTY

Mix ingredients in a shaker with crushed ice. Pour into glass and garnish with the pineapple and coconut.

SOUTH SEA DREAM

- Highball/Collins glass
- Shaker
- 3/4 ounce cream of coconut
- 3/4 ounce pineapple juice
- 1 ounce Pisang Ambon
- 3/4 ounce light rum
- 2 tsp. light cream

GARNISH
- 1/4 slice of pineapple
- 1 maraschino cherry
- Sprig of mint

SWEET, LONG DRINK FOR THE SUMMER

Shake all the ingredients together firmly, with ice, in the shaker and strain into the highball glass over ice. Perch the piece of pineapple on the rim of the glass and fasten the cherry to it with a toothpick. Add the sprig of mint to the glass.

CHOCOLATE COCO

- Large brandy snifter with a coconut-coated rim
- Shaker
- 2 ounces pineapple juice
- 1 ounce Malibu or other coconut-flavored liqueur
- 1 ounce light rum
- 3/4 ounce lemon juice
- 3/4 ounce chocolate sauce

MILD DRINK FOR A SUMMER PARTY

Shake all the ingredients together, with ice, in the shaker and pour into the snifter.

Blue Hawaiian

RUM

Red Colada

- Highball/Collins glass
- Shaker
- 1 3/4 ounces cream of coconut
- 1 3/4 ounces pineapple juice
- 1 ounce light rum
- 1 ounce orange curaçao
- 2 tsp. light cream

GARNISH
- 1/4 slice of pineapple
- 1 maraschino cherry

Shake the ingredients together firmly, with ice, in the shaker and strain into the highball glass over crushed ice. Perch the fruit on the rim of the glass.

Con Tico

SPICY, SWEET DRINK FOR ANY TIME OF THE YEAR

- Highball/Collins glass
- Shaker
- 1 3/4 ounces pineapple juice
- 1 ounce light rum
- 2 tsp. Southern Comfort
- 2 tsp. Cointreau or other orange-flavored liqueur
- 2 tsp. Cinzano (rosso antico)

GARNISH
- 1/4 slice of pineapple
- 1 slice of orange
- 1 maraschino cherry

Shake all the ingredients together well, with ice cubes, in the shaker and strain into the highball glass. Finally perch the fruit on the rim of the glass.

Looking At You

SPICY, MILD DRINK FOR THE SUMMER

- Highball/Collins glass with a sugared rim
- Shaker
- 3 1/2 ounces orange juice
- 1 ounce Sambuca
- 3/4 ounce light rum
- 2 tsp. dark rum

GARNISH
- 1 slice of orange
- 1 maraschino cherry

Shake all the ingredients together, with ice cubes, in the shaker and strain into the glass. Top up with crushed ice. Perch the fruit on the rim of the glass.

COLT CRUISER

LIGHT, LONG DRINK FOR HOT DAYS

- Highball/Collins glass
- Shaker
- 3/4 ounce light rum
- 3/4 ounce lemon juice
- 2 tsp. crème de banane
- 2 tsp. amaretto
- Lemonade for topping up
GARNISH
- 1 piece of orange peel
- 1 maraschino cherry

Shake all the ingredients, except the lemonade, together, with ice, in the shaker and strain into the highball glass over ice cubes. Top up with lemonade and stir. Put the orange peel and cherry in the glass and serve the drink with a stirrer.

FOUR FLUSH

MILD, SPICY DRINK FOR ANY TIME OF THE YEAR

- Cocktail glass
- Mixing glass
- 1 ounce light rum
- 3/4 ounce dry vermouth
- 2 tsp. maraschino
- 2 dashes grenadine
GARNISH
- 1 maraschino cherry

Mix all the ingredients together, with ice cubes, in the mixing glass and strain into the glass. Spear the cherry on a toothpick and add it to the glass.

A LULU

FRUITY, MILD DRINK FOR A PARTY

- Rocks glass
- Shaker
- 1 1/2 ounces light rum
- 1 ounce passion-fruit juice
- 1 ounce orange juice
- 3/4 ounce nut-flavored liqueur

Shake all the ingredients together, with ice, in the shaker and pour into the glass. Serve with a straw.

PINA COLADA

SWEET DRINK FOR A SUMMER PARTY

- Highball/Collins glass
- Shaker
- 1 3/4 ounces cream of coconut
- 1 3/4 ounces pineapple juice
- 1 1/2 ounces light rum
- 2 tsp. light cream

GARNISH
- Slices of orange

Shake all the ingredients together firmly, with ice, in the shaker and strain into the highball glass over crushed ice. Garnish with fanned orange slices.

GOLDEN COLADA

FRUITY, MILD LONG DRINK FOR A SUMMER PARTY

- Highball/Collins glass
- Shaker
- 1 ounce dark rum
- 3/4 ounce light rum
- 3/4 ounce cream of coconut
- 3/4 ounce orange juice
- 3/4 ounce pineapple juice
- 2 tsp. Galliano
- 2 tsp. light cream

GARNISH
- 1/2 slice of pineapple
- 1 maraschino cherry

Shake all the ingredients together firmly, with ice cubes, in the shaker and strain into the highball glass, half filled with crushed ice. Spear the slice of pineapple and the cherry on a toothpick and lay the garnish across the rim of the glass.

SEPTEMBER MORNING

FRUITY, MILD DRINK FOR ANY TIME OF THE YEAR

- Large brandy snifter
- Shaker
- 2 ounces light rum
- 3/4 ounce lime juice
- 2 tsp. grenadine
- 1 egg white

Shake all the ingredients together firmly in the shaker and pour carefully into the brandy snifter.

Pina Colada

RUM

EYE-OPENER

STRONG, SHORT DRINK FOR THE EVENING

- Sour glass
- Shaker
- 2 ounces light rum
- 1 tsp. Pernod
- 1 tsp. Cointreau
- 1 tsp. white crème de cacao
- 1/2 tsp. sugar
- 1 egg yolk

Shake all ingredients vigorously with cracked ice in a shaker. Strain into chilled sour glass.

FERN GULLY

EXOTIC COCKTAIL FOR SUMMER

- Red wine glass
- Shaker
- 2 ounces dark rum
- 1 1/2 ounces light rum
- 1/2 ounce amaretto
- 1/2 ounce coconut cream
- 1 ounce orange juice
- 1 ounce fresh lime juice

Combine all ingredients, with crushed ice, in a shaker. Shake and pour into glass.

FORT LAUDERDALE

SOUR DRINK FOR THE EVENING

- Old-fashioned glass
- Shaker
- 2 ounce light rum
- 1/2 ounce sweet vermouth
- 1 ounce fresh lime juice
- 1 ounce orange juice
GARNISH
- 1 slice of orange

Combine all ingredients, with cracked ice, in a shaker. Shake well and strain into chilled old-fashioned glass over ice cubes. Garnish with orange.

HAVANA CLUB

- Cocktail glass
- Mixing glass
- 1 1/2 ounces light rum
- 3/4 ounce sweet red vermouth
- Extra: 1 lemon peel piece

SPICY, MILD APERITIF

Mix all the ingredients together, with ice cubes, in the mixing glass and strain into the glass. Squeeze the lemon peel over the drink.

BEACH

- Cocktail glass
- Shaker
- 1 1/2 ounces light rum
- 3/4 ounce white crème de menthe
- 2 tsp. lemon juice

FRUITY DRINK FOR HOT DAYS

Shake all the ingredients together firmly, with ice, in the shaker and strain into the glass.

BEAU RIVAGE

- Large cocktail glass
- Shaker
- 1 ounce orange juice
- 3/4 ounce light rum
- 3/4 ounce gin
- 2 tsp. dry vermouth
- 2 tsp. sweet red vermouth
- 1 dash grenadine

FRUITY, MILD SHORT DRINK FOR ANY TIME OF YEAR

Shake all the ingredients together, with ice cubes, in the shaker and strain into the cocktail glass.

RUM

MARUMBA

- Rocks glass
- Shaker
- 3/4 ounce dark rum
- 3/4 ounce mandarin-flavored liqueur
- Juice of 1/2 lemon

GARNISH
- 1 mandarin peel spiral
- Mandarin segments

FRUITY, BITTER DRINK

Put the ingredients, with ice, in a shaker, shake well and then strain into a glass. Garnish with fruit.

BLUE BOY

- Cocktail glass
- Mixing glass
- 1 ounce light rum
- 1 ounce sweet red vermouth
- 1 dash orange bitters
- 1 dash Angostura bitters
- Extra: 1 piece of lemon peel

SPICY APERITIF

Mix all the ingredients together, with ice, in the mixing glass and strain into the cocktail glass. Squeeze the lemon peel over the drink and add the peel to the glass.

AMARO

- Sherry glass
- Mixing glass
- 1 1/2 ounces light rum
- 3/4 ounce amaretto

GARNISH
- 1 piece of lemon peel
- 1 tsp. coffee powder

BITTERSWEET AFTER-DINNER DRINK

Mix the ingredients together, with ice cubes, in the mixing glass and pour into the sherry glass. Perch the slice of lemon on the rim of the glass and dust with coffee powder.

Marumba

RUM

YELLOW BIRD

- Cocktail glass
- Shaker
- 1 ounce white rum
- 1/3 ounce Galliano
- 1/3 ounce Cointreau
- 1/3 ounce fresh lime juice

GARNISH
- 1 slice lime

SWEET APERITIF OR AFTER-DINNER DRINK

Shake all the ingredients in the shaker and strain into a cocktail glass. Garnish with lime.

DREAM

- Cocktail glass
- Shaker
- 3/4 ounce light rum
- 3/4 ounce crème de banane
- 2 tsp. pineapple juice
- 2 tsp. light cream
- 1 dash grenadine

CREAMY AFTER-DINNER DRINK

Shake the ingredients together firmly, with ice, in the shaker and strain into the cocktail glass.

WINDJAMMER

- Cocktail glass with a sugared rim
- Mixing glass
- 1 1/2 ounces light rum
- 3/4 ounce dry vermouth
- 2 tsp. grenadine

GARNISH
- 2 maraschino cherries

SPICY, MILD DRINK FOR A PARTY

Shake all the ingredients together, with ice cubes, in the shaker and strain into the cocktail glass with the sugared rim. Add the cherries to the glass.

Yellow Bird

WHISKEY-BASED DRINKS

WHISKEY

ROB ROY

AROMATIC DRINK

- Cocktail glass
- Mixing glass
- 1 1/2 ounces scotch
- 3/4 ounce sweet red vermouth
- 1 dash Angostura bitters

GARNISH
- 1 maraschino cherry

Mix the ingredients together, with ice, in the mixing glass and strain into the cocktail glass. Spear the cherry on a toothpick and add it to the glass.

CONTINENTAL SOUR

FRUITY, MILD, DRY SOUR FOR THE EVENING

- Rocks glass
- Shaker
- 1 3/4 ounces bourbon
- 1 ounce grenadine
- 3/4 ounce lemon juice
- 1 egg white
- 1 dash red wine

GARNISH
- 1 slice of orange

Shake all the ingredients, except the red wine, together well, with ice, in the shaker and strain into the glass. Add the red wine and stir. Perch the slice of orange on the rim of the glass.

NEW YORKER

FRUITY APERITIF

- Cocktail glass
- Shaker
- 1 1/2 ounces bourbon
- 3/4 ounce lemon juice
- 2 tsp. grenadine

Shake all the ingredients together, with ice, in the shaker and strain into the cocktail glass.

JOKER

- Cocktail glass
- Mixing glass
- 1 ounce scotch
- $1/2$ ounce Grand Marnier
- $1/2$ ounce Dubonnet

AROMATIC DRINK

Stir the ingredients together, with ice, in the mixing glass and strain into the cocktail glass.

CHURCHILL

- Cocktail glass
- Shaker
- 2 ounces scotch
- 3/4 ounce sweet red vermouth
- 1 dash triple sec
- 1 dash lemon juice

GARNISH
- 1 slice of lemon

DELICATE, DRY DRINK FOR THE EVENING

Shake all the ingredients together, with ice, in the shaker and strain into the cocktail glass. Perch the slice of lemon on the rim of the glass.

MONTE CARLO

- Cocktail glass
- Mixing glass
- $1 1/2$ ounces bourbon
- 3/4 ounce Benedictine
- 1 dash Angostura bitters

DELICATE, DRY AFTER-DINNER DRINK

Stir all the ingredients together, with ice, in the mixing glass and strain into the cocktail glass.

WHISKEY

RUSTY NAIL

- Rocks glass
- 1 ounce scotch
- 1 ounce Drambuie

SWEET AFTER-DINNER DRINK

Mix all the ingredients together in the glass, with ice cubes, and stir with a stirrer.

LORD BYRON

- Rocks glass
- Mixing glass
- 1 ounce scotch
- 2 tsp. orange-flavored liqueur
- 2 tsp. sweet red vermouth
- 1 dash Angostura bitters
GARNISH
- 1 slice of orange

SPICY, FRUITY DRINK FOR THE EVENING

Stir all the ingredients together, with ice, in the mixing glass and strain into the glass. Add the slice of orange to the glass. Serve immediately.

GOLDEN NAIL

- Rocks glass
- 1 ounce bourbon
- 3/4 ounce Southern Comfort

FRUITY, SPICY AFTER-DINNER DRINK

Mix all the ingredients together in the glass with ice cubes.

Rusty Nail

WHISKEY

TENNESSEE

FRUITY, DELICATELY DRY DRINK FOR THE EVENING

- Cocktail glass
- Shaker
- 1½ ounces bourbon
- 2 tsp. maraschino
- 1 dash lemon juice

GARNISH
- 1 maraschino cherry

Shake all the ingredients together, with ice, in the shaker and strain into the cocktail glass. Perch the cherry on the rim of the glass.

MISSOURI MULE

FRUITY, DELICATELY DRY DRINK FOR THE EVENING

- Cocktail glass
- Shaker
- 1½ ounces bourbon
- 2 tsp. crème de cassis
- 2 tsp. lemon juice

GARNISH
- 1 slice of lemon

Shake all the ingredients together firmly, with ice, in the shaker and strain into the cocktail glass. Perch the lemon on the rim of the glass.

OLD PALE

SPICY, DRY DRINK FOR THE EVENING OR AS AN APERITIF

- Cocktail glass with sugared rim
- Mixing glass
- 1 ounce bourbon
- ¾ ounce Campari
- 1 tsp. lime syrup
- Extra: 1 piece of lemon peel

Stir all the ingredients together, with ice, in the mixing glass and strain into the cocktail glass. Add the piece of lemon peel to the glass.

BROOKLYN

- Cocktail glass
- Mixing glass
- 1 1/2 ounces Canadian whiskey
- 3/4 ounce dry vermouth
- 2 dashes maraschino

DRY, SPICY APERITIF

Stir all the ingredients together, with ice, in the mixing glass and strain into the glass.

BOURBON CAR

- Cocktail glass
- Shaker
- 1 1/2 ounces bourbon
- 3/4 ounce Cointreau or other orange-flavored liqueur
- 3/4 ounce lemon juice
GARNISH
- 1 maraschino cherry

FRUITY, SOURISH DRINK FOR THE EVENING

Shake all the ingredients together, with crushed ice, in the shaker and pour into the cocktail glass. Perch the cherry on the rim of the glass.

PIERRE

- Cocktail glass
- Mixing glass
- 1 ounce bourbon
- 3/4 ounce apricot brandy
- 2 tsp. lemon juice
- Extra: 1 piece of lemon peel

DELICATE, DRY DRINK FOR THE EVENING

Mix all the ingredients together, with ice, in the mixing glass and strain into the cocktail glass. Add the lemon peel to the glass.

WHISKEY

OLD-FASHIONED BOURBON

- Old-fashioned glass
- 1 sugar lump
- 3 dashes Angostura bitters
- 1 1/2 ounces bourbon
- Water or still mineral water

GARNISH
- 1/2 slice of lemon (optional)
- 1/2 slice of orange
- 2 maraschino cherries (optional)

STRONG APERITIF

Put the sugar lump in the glass, drizzle the Angostura bitters over it, and crush it. Add a few ice cubes to the glass and pour the bourbon over them. Add a little water and stir. Add the fruit to the glass. Serve with a stirrer.

IRISH ROSE

- Cocktail glass
- Shaker
- 1 1/2 ounces Irish whiskey
- 3/4 ounce lemon juice
- 2 tsp. Grenadine

STRONG APERITIF

Shake the ingredients together, with ice, in the shaker and strain into the cocktail glass.

HANDLEBAR

- Cocktail glass
- Shaker
- 1 ounce scotch
- 2 tsp. Drambuie
- 2 tsp. lime juice

DRY DRINK FOR THE EVENING

Shake all the ingredients together, with ice, in the shaker and strain into the glass.

Old-Fashioned Bourbon

WHISKEY

LAFAYETTE

- Cocktail glass
- Mixing glass
- 1 ounce bourbon
- 2 tsp. dry vermouth
- 2 tsp. Dubonnet
- 2 dashes Angostura bitters

DELICATE, DRY APERITIF

Stir all the ingredients together, with ice, in the mixing glass and strain into the cocktail glass.

KENTUCKY BOURBON

- Cocktail glass
- Mixing glass
- 1 1/2 ounces bourbon
- 3/4 ounce Benedictine

GARNISH
- 1 maraschino cherry

DELICATE, DRY AFTER-DINNER DRINK

Stir all the ingredients together, with ice, in the mixing glass and strain into the cocktail glass. Perch the cherry on the rim of the glass.

DON JOSÉ

- Cocktail glass
- Shaker
- 3/4 ounce bourbon
- 3/4 ounce sweet red vermouth
- 2 tsp. banana-flavored liqueur

SPICY, SHORT DRINK FOR THE EVENING

Shake all of the ingredients together, with crushed ice, in the shaker and pour into the cocktail glass.

DELTA

- Rocks glass
- Shaker
- 1 ounce bourbon
- 2 tsp. Southern Comfort
- 2 tsp. lime syrup

GARNISH
- 1/2 slice of orange
- 1 maraschino cherry

FRUITY, SWEET DRINK FOR THE EVENING

Shake all of the ingredients together well, with ice, in the shaker and strain into the glass half filled with crushed ice. Perch the fruit on the rim of the glass.

RITZ OLD-FASHIONED

- Old-fashioned glass with sugared rim
- Shaker
- 1 1/2 ounces bourbon
- 3/4 ounce Grand Marnier
- 1 dash lemon juice
- 1 dash maraschino

FRUITY, MILD DRINK FOR THE EVENING

Shake all the ingredients together, with ice, in the shaker and strain into the glass.

AMERICA

- Cocktail glass
- Shaker
- 1 3/4 ounces bourbon
- 1/2 ounce lime juice
- 2 tsp. grenadine
- Extra: 1 piece of lime peel

DELICATE, DRY DRINK FOR THE EVENING

Shake all the ingredients together, with ice, in the shaker and strain into the glass. Squeeze the lime peel over the drink and add it to the glass.

WHISKEY

MANHATTAN

- Cocktail glass
- Mixing glass
- 1 1/2 ounces Canadian whiskey
- 3/4 ounce sweet red vermouth
- 1 dash Angostura bitters
- Extra: 1 maraschino cherry
- 1 piece of lemon peel (optional)

CLASSIC APERITIF

Stir the ingredients together in the mixing glass, with ice, and strain into the cocktail glass. Spear the cherry on a toothpick, put it in the drink, and squeeze the lemon peel over the drink, if liked.

DRY MANHATTAN

- Cocktail glass
- Mixing glass
- 1 1/2 ounces Canadian whiskey
- 3/4 ounce dry vermouth
- Extra: 1 green olive
- 1 piece of lemon peel (optional)

CLASSIC APERITIF

Stir the ingredients together in the mixing glass, with ice, and strain into the cocktail glass. Spear the olive on a toothpick, put it in the drink, and squeeze the lemon peel over the drink, if liked.

PERFECT MANHATTAN

- Cocktail glass
- Mixing glass
- 1 1/2 ounces bourbon
- 2 tsp. dry vermouth
- 2 tsp. sweet red vermouth

AROMATIC DRINK FOR THE EVENING

Stir the ingredients together in the mixing glass, with ice, and strain into the cocktail glass.

Manhattan

WHISKEY

HAWK

FRUITY, DRY DRINK FOR THE EVENING

- Cocktail glass
- Shaker
- 3/4 ounce bourbon
- 3/4 ounce gin
- 2 tsp. lemon juice

GARNISH
- 1 maraschino cherry

Shake all the ingredients together, with ice, in the shaker and strain into the glass. Perch the cherry on the rim of the glass.

BISHOP

FRUITY, DELICATE, TANGY DRINK FOR THE EVENING

- Cocktail glass
- Shaker
- 1 ounce Canadian whiskey
- 2 tsp. sweet red vermouth
- 2 tsp. orange juice
- 1 tsp. green Chartreuse

Shake all the ingredients together, with ice, in the shaker and strain into the glass.

CANADA

FRUITY MILD DRINK FOR THE EVENING

- Cocktail glass
- Shaker
- 1 ounce Canadian whiskey
- 2 tsp. triple sec
- 2 tsp. maple syrup
- 2 dashes Angostura bitters

Shake all the ingredients together, with ice, in the shaker and strain into the cocktail glass.

WHISKEY TWIST

- Cocktail glass
- Mixing glass
- 1 1/2 ounces Irish whiskey
- 2 tsp. lemon juice
- 1 tsp. cherry brandy
- 1 tsp. raspberry syrup

GARNISH
- 1 maraschino cherry

FRUITY, SLIGHTLY SOUR DRINK FOR THE EVENING

Stir all the ingredients together, with ice cubes, in the mixing glass and strain into the cocktail glass. Perch the cherry on the rim of the glass.

4TH OF JULY

- Rocks glass
- Shaker
- 1 3/4 ounces orange juice
- 1 ounce bourbon
- 2 tsp. apricot brandy
- 2 tsp. lemon juice

GARNISH
- 1 slice of orange
- 1 slice of lemon

FRUITY, SLIGHTLY DRY DRINK FOR THE EVENING

Shake all the ingredients together well, with ice cubes, in the shaker and strain into the glass. Perch the fruit on the rim of the glass.

YORK

- Cocktail glass
- Mixing glass
- 2 ounces bourbon
- 3/4 ounce sweet red vermouth
- 3 dashes Angostura bitters

GARNISH
- 1 maraschino cherry

DELICATE, DRY DRINK FOR THE EVENING

Mix all the ingredients together, with ice, in the mixing glass and strain into the cocktail glass. Perch the cherry on the rim of the glass.

WHISKEY

BLOOD AND SAND

- Cocktail glass
- Shaker
- 1 ounce whiskey
- 1/2 ounce cherry brandy
- 1/2 ounce sweet vermouth
- 1 ounce orange juice

GARNISH
- 1 slice of orange

FRUITY DRINK FOR A PARTY

Shake all the ingredients together in the shaker with the cracked ice. Strain and pour into the glass. Garnish with the slice of orange.

BOURBON HIGHBALL

- Highball/Collins glass
- 1 1/2 ounces bourbon
- 1 piece of lemon peel
- Ginger ale for topping up

GARNISH
- 1 lemon peel spiral

SWEET, SPICY DRINK FOR ANY TIME OF THE YEAR

Put the whiskey in the glass with ice cubes. Squeeze the lemon peel over the whiskey and add it to the glass. Top up with ginger ale. Hang the lemon peel spiral over the rim of the glass.

WHISKEY SOUR

- Sour glass
- Mixing glass
- 1 1/2 ounces bourbon
- 3/4 ounce lemon juice
- 2 tsp. sugar syrup
- 1 dash Angostura bitters

GARNISH
- 1/2 slice of orange
- 1 maraschino cherry

REFRESHING SOUR FOR THE EVENING

Shake all the ingredients together, with ice, in the shaker and strain into the glass. Perch the fruit on the rim of the glass.

Blood and Sand

WHISKEY

CANADIAN SOUR

- Rocks glass
- Shaker
- 1 1/2 ounces Canadian whiskey
- 3/4 ounce lemon juice
- 2 tsp. sugar syrup
- Sparkling mineral water (optional)

GARNISH
- 1/2 slice of orange
- 1 orange peel spiral
- 1 maraschino cherry

REFRESHING DRINK FOR A PARTY

Shake all the ingredients together, with ice, in the shaker and strain into the glass. Add a little mineral water. Perch the slice of orange on the rim of the glass; spear the cherry and orange peel spiral with a toothpick and insert it into the slice of orange. Add to the drink.

19TH HOLE

- Highball/Collins glass
- Shaker
- 2 3/4 ounces passion-fruit juice
- 1 ounce scotch
- 3/4 ounce Southern Comfort
- 2 tsp. mandarin syrup
- 2 tsp. lemon juice

GARNISH
- 1 Cape gooseberry

REFRESHING, FRUITY DRINK FOR A SUMMER PARTY

Shake the ingredients together, with ice, in the shaker and strain into the highball/Collins glass over crushed ice. Perch the Cape gooseberry on the rim of the glass.

WALDORF ASTORIA

- Rocks glass
- Shaker
- 3 1/2 ounces milk
- 1 1/2 ounces bourbon
- 3/4 ounce port
- 2 tsp. sugar syrup
- 2 tsp. light cream
- 2 egg yolks
- Extra: Grated nutmeg

STRONG, SWEET EGGNOG FOR EVERY DAY

Shake the ingredients together very firmly, with ice, in the shaker and pour into the glass. Sprinkle a little grated nutmeg on top.

BLUEGRASS

- Highball/Collins glass
- Shaker
- 1 ounce bourbon
- 1 ounce lemon juice
- 3/4 ounce lime juice
- 1/2 ounce blue curaçao
- 1/2 ounce Southern Comfort

GARNISH
- 1 piece of lemon peel
- 1 maraschino cherry

AROMATIC DRINK FOR A PARTY

Shake the ingredients together, with ice, in the shaker and strain into the highball/Collins glass with ice. Add the lemon peel and maraschino cherry to the glass.

COLONEL COLLINS

- Collins/Highball glass
- 2 ounces bourbon
- 1 ounce lemon juice
- 3/4 ounce sugar syrup
- Soda water for topping up

GARNISH
- 1 slice of lemon
- 1 maraschino cherry

FRUITY, SWEET-AND-SOUR COLLINS FOR THE SUMMER

Mix together the bourbon, lemon juice, and sugar syrup, with ice cubes, in the Collins glass. Top up with the soda water and stir briefly. Perch the slice of lemon on the rim of the glass and fasten the cherry to it with a toothpick.

WHISKEY SLING

- Large rocks glass
- 1 1/2 ounces bourbon
- 1 1/2 ounces sugar syrup
- 3/4 ounce lemon juice
- Soda water

FRUITY, MILD DRINK FOR A SUMMER'S EVENING

Mix together the bourbon, sugar syrup, and lemon juice, with ice cubes, in the glass. Top up with the soda water and stir briefly.

WHISKEY

IRISH COCKTAIL

- Cocktail glass
- Shaker
- 1 ounce Irish whiskey
- 6 dashes crème de menthe
- 3 dashes green Chartreuse

GARNISH
- 2 maraschino cherries

LIGHT DRINK FOR THE EVENING

Pour the whiskey, crème de menthe and Chartreuse into a cocktail shaker with a scoop of ice cubes. Shake and strain into a cocktail glass. Garnish with the cherries on a toothpick.

LOS ANGELES

- Highball/Collins glass
- Shaker
- 1 ounce scotch
- 3/4 ounce lemon juice
- 2 tsp. sugar syrup
- 1 dash sweet white vermouth
- 1 egg

FRUITY DRINK FOR A PARTY

Shake the ingredients together firmly, with ice, in the shaker and strain into the Highball/Collins glass.

IRISH ORANGE

- Large rocks glass
- Shaker
- 1 1/2 ounces Irish whiskey
- 2 tsp. lemon juice
- 2 tsp. grenadine
- Bitter orange for topping up

GARNISH
- 1 orange peel spiral

FRUITY, DRY DRINK FOR THE EVENING

Shake all the ingredients, except the bitter orange, together, with ice, in the shaker and strain into the glass over ice cubes. Top up with bitter orange and stir. Hang the orange peel spiral over the rim of the glass.

Irish Cocktail

WHISKEY

GODFATHER

SWEET SHORT DRINK FOR ANY OCCASION

- Rocks glass
- 1 3/4 ounces bourbon
- 3/4 ounce amaretto

Mix all the ingredients together in the glass, with ice, and serve the drink with a stirrer.

SCOTCH RICKEY

FRUITY, SLIGHTLY SOUR DRINK FOR THE EVENING

- Highball/Collins glass
- Shaker
- 1 1/2 ounces scotch
- 2 tsp. lemon juice
- 2 tsp. lime cordial
- Soda water for topping up
GARNISH
- 1 slice of lemon
- 1 slice of lime

Shake all the ingredients, except the soda water, with ice, in the shaker and strain into the glass. Top up with the soda water and stir briefly. Perch the slices of fruit on the rim of the glass.

HOLIDAY EGGNOG

SWEET EGGNOG ALSO ENJOYABLE THROUGHOUT THE YEAR

- Highball/Collins glass
- Shaker
- 1 1/2 ounces bourbon
- 1 1/2 ounces milk
- 3/4 ounce dark rum
- 2 tsp. sugar syrup
- 1 egg
- Extra: grated nutmeg

Shake all the ingredients together, with ice, in the shaker and strain into the glass. Sprinkle with a little grated nutmeg.

SANDY COLLINS

REFRESHING COLLINS FOR ANY TIME OF DAY

- Highball/Collins glass
- 1 1/2 ounces scotch
- 3/4 ounce lemon juice
- 2 tsp. sugar syrup
- Soda water for topping up

GARNISH
- 1/2 slice of lemon
- 1 maraschino cherry

Mix all the ingredients, except the soda water, together, with ice, in the highball/Collins glass. Top up with the soda water and stir until the glass condenses. Spear the fruit on a toothpick and lay the garnish across the rim of the glass.

FREEFALL

FRUITY DRINK FOR A SUMMER PARTY

- Highball/Collins glass
- Shaker
- 2 ounces pineapple juice
- 1 ounce scotch
- 3/4 ounce Malibu or other coconut-flavored liqueur
- 2 tsp. passion-fruit syrup
- 2 tsp. lemon juice

GARNISH
- 1 piece of pineapple
- 1 maraschino cherry

Shake all the ingredients together, with ice, in the shaker and strain into the highball/Collins glass with ice cubes. Spear the fruit on a toothpick and lay across the rim of the glass.

BOURBON SILVER FIZZ

FRUITY, DELICATE DRY DRINK FOR THE AFTERNOON AND EVENING

- Large rocks glass
- Shaker
- 1 ounce bourbon
- 1 tsp. lemon juice
- 1 tsp. lime juice
- 1 tsp. sugar syrup
- 1 egg white
- Soda water for topping up

GARNISH
- 1 slice of lemon

Shake all the ingredients together, with ice, in the shaker and strain into the glass. Top up with soda water and stir. Perch the lemon on the rim of the glass.

WHISKEY

DANDY

- Cocktail glass
- Mixing glass
- 1 ounce rye
- 1 ounce Dubonnet
- 3 dashes Angostura bitters
- 1 dash lemon juice
- Extra: Lemon and orange peel (optional)

AROMATIC APERITIF

Mix the ingredients together, with ice, in the mixing glass and strain into the cocktail glass. Squeeze the lemon and orange peel over the drink and add the peels to the glass.

KING'S CROSS

- Cocktail glass
- Mixing glass
- 1 ounce bourbon
- 1 ounce sweet red vermouth
- 1 dash Benedictine
- Extra: 1 piece of lemon peel

MEDIUM-DRY APERITIF

Shake the ingredients together, with ice, in the shaker and strain into the cocktail glass. Squeeze the lemon peel over the drink and add the peel to the glass.

OLYMPIA

- Cocktail glass
- Shaker
- 1/2 ounce Canadian whiskey
- 1/2 ounce dry vermouth
- 2 tsp. green Chartreuse
- 2 tsp. Escorial or other herb-flavored liqueur
- 2 tsp. greengage cordial

GARNISH
- 1 black grape

SWEET APERITIF OR AFTER-DINNER DRINK

Shake the ingredients together, with ice, in the shaker and strain into the cocktail glass. Put the grape in the glass.

Dandy

WHISKEY

CHAMPION

- Cocktail glass
- Mixing glass
- 3/4 ounce scotch
- 3/4 ounce dry vermouth
- 2 tsp. Benedectine
- 2 tsp. triple sec

MEDIUM-DRY DRINK FOR PARTIES

Stir the ingredients together, with ice, in the mixing glass and strain into the glass.

TUTIOSI

- Cocktail glass
- Mixing glass
- 3/4 ounce Canadian whiskey
- 1/2 ounce brandy
- 1/2 ounce sweet red vermouth
- 2 tsp. Galliano
- 2 tsp. mandarin-flavored liqueur
- Extra: 1 piece of orange peel

SWEET AFTER-DINNER DRINK

Stir the ingredients together, with ice, in the mixing glass and strain into the glass. Squeeze the orange peel over the drink and add the peel to it.

NEW YORK FLIP

- Cocktail glass
- Shaker
- 1 ounce bourbon
- 3/4 ounce port
- 3/4 ounce light cream
- 2 tsp. sugar syrup
- 1 egg yolk
- Extra: Grated nutmeg

SWEET AFTER-DINNER DRINK

Shake the ingredients together very firmly, with ice, in the shaker and strain into the cocktail glass. Sprinkle a little nutmeg over the drink and serve immediately.

IZCARAGUA

- Cocktail glass
- Mixing glass
- $1/2$ ounce scotch
- $1/2$ ounce dry vermouth
- $1/2$ ounce amaretto
- $1/2$ ounce crème de banane
- Extra: 1 piece of lemon peel

MEDIUM-DRY AFTER-DINNER DRINK

Stir all the ingredients together, with ice, in the mixing glass and strain into the cocktail glass. Add the lemon peel to the glass.

UNION CLUB

- Cocktail glass
- Shaker
- $1 1/2$ ounces bourbon
- $3/4$ ounce triple sec
- $3/4$ ounce lemon juice
- 1 tsp. egg white
- 2 dashes grenadine

FRUITY, DRY DRINK FOR THE EVENING

Shake all the ingredients together, with ice, in the shaker and strain into the glass.

CREOLE

- Cocktail glass
- Mixing glass
- $3/4$ ounce bourbon
- $3/4$ ounce sweet red vermouth
- 2 tsp. Benedictine

GARNISH
- 1 slice of lemon

MILD, SPICY DRINK FOR THE EVENING

Stir all the ingredients together, with ice, in the mixing glass and strain into the glass. Perch the slice of lemon on the rim of the glass.

WHISKEY

BARBERA

- Rocks glass
- Shaker
- 1 ounce bourbon
- 3/4 ounce Drambuie
- 1/2 ounce amaretto
- 2 dashes orange bitters

GARNISH
- 1 piece of lemon peel spiral (optional)
- Orange slices

BITTER, SHORT DRINK

Put the ingredients in the shaker, with ice, and shake firmly. Strain into the glass and squeeze the orange rind into the drink. Garnish with fruit.

ERANS

- Cocktail glass
- Mixing glass
- 1 1/2 ounces bourbon
- 2 tsp. apricot brandy
- 2 tsp. Cointreau or other orange-flavored liqueur

FRUITY, SWEET DRINK FOR THE EVENING

Stir all the ingredients together, with ice, in the mixing glass and strain into the cocktail glass.

HIGHLAND FLING

- Rocks glass
- Mixing glass
- 1 ounce scotch
- 1 ounce Drambuie

GARNISH
- 1 slice of lemon
- 1 maraschino cherry

SPICY, MILD DRINK FOR THE EVENING

Stir all the ingredients together, with ice, in the mixing glass and strain into the glass. Spear the fruit on a toothpick and balance across the rim of the glass.

Barbera

WHISKEY

BOURBON SKIN

- Cocktail glass
- Shaker
- 1 3/4 ounces bourbon
- 3/4 ounce lemon juice
- 1 tsp. grenadine
GARNISH
- 1 maraschino cherry

FRUITY, DRY DRINK FOR THE EVENING

Shake all the ingredients together, with crushed ice, in the shaker and pour into the cocktail glass. Perch the cherry on the rim of the glass.

BARBICANE

- Cocktail glass
- Shaker
- 1 ounce scotch
- 1 ounce passion-fruit nectar
- 2 tsp. Drambuie
- 1 dash lemon juice
GARNISH
- 1 maraschino cherry

FRUITY, MILD DRINK FOR A PARTY

Shake all the ingredients together, with ice cubes, in the shaker and strain into the cocktail glass. Perch the cherry on the rim of the glass.

COWBOY

- Cocktail glass
- Shaker
- 1 1/2 ounces bourbon
- 3/4 ounce light cream

CREAMY, AFTER-DINNER DRINK

Shake all the ingredients together, with ice, in the shaker and strain into the glass.

GOLDEN GLOW

- Cocktail glass
- Shaker
- 2 ounces bourbon
- I ounce dark rum
- 2 ounces orange juice
- I tbsp. lemon juice
- 1/2 tsp. sugar syrup
- I dash grenadine

FRUITY, MILD DRINK FOR A PARTY

Combine all ingredients, except the grenadine, with cracked ice in a cocktail shaker. Shake well and strain into a chilled cocktail glass. Float grenadine on top.

HAWAIIAN EYE

- Old-fashioned glass
- Blender
- 2 ounces bourbon
- I ounce vodka
- I ounce coffee liqueur
- 1/2 ounce Pernod
- I ounce half-and-half
- 2 ounces maraschino
- I egg white

GARNISH
- I maraschino cherry
- I pineapple spear

RICH, AFTER-DINNER DRINK

Combine all the ingredients, with cracked ice, in a blender. Blend until smooth and pour into glass. Garnish with fruit.

KING COLE

- Old-fashioned glass
- 2 ounces scotch
- I orange slice
- I pineapple slice
- 1/2 tsp. sugar

REFRESHING DRINK FOR A PARTY

Muddle fruit and sugar in an old-fashioned glass. Add whiskey and ice cubes. Stir well.

WHISKEY

CAPRICORN

- Rocks glass
- Shaker
- 1 ounce bourbon whiskey
- 1/2 ounce apricot brandy
- 2 ounces orange juice
- 1/2 ounce lemon juice

GARNISH
- 1 orange slice

FRUITY, SWEET DRINK

Shake the ingredients together, with ice, in a shaker and strain into the glass. Garnish with the orange slice.

ESQUIRE MANHATTAN

- Cocktail glass
- Mixing glass
- 3/4 ounce bourbon
- 3/4 ounce sweet red vermouth
- 1 dash orange bitters

GARNISH
- 1 green maraschino cherry

DELICATE, DRY APERITIF

Stir the ingredients together, with ice, in the mixing glass and strain into the cocktail glass. Perch the cherry on the rim of the glass.

QUATTRO

- Cocktail glass
- Mixing glass
- 1/2 ounce Canadian whiskey
- 1/2 ounce amaretto
- 1/2 ounce crème de cassis
- 1/2 ounce dry vermouth

GARNISH
- 1 maraschino cherry
- 1 piece of orange peel

AROMATIC APERITIF OR AFTER-DINNER DRINK

Stir the ingredients together, with ice, in the mixing glass and strain into the cocktail glass. Add the cherry and the piece of orange peel to the glass.

Capricorn

WHISKEY

BLINKER

FRUITY APERITIF

- Cocktail glass
- Shaker
- 1 ounce Canadian whiskey
- 1 ounce grapefruit juice
- 3/4 ounce grenadine

Shake all the ingredients together, with ice, in the shaker and strain into the glass.

SAZERAC

STRONG, ANISEED-FLAVORED APERITIF

- Cocktail glass
- Mixing glass
- 3/4 ounce scotch
- 3/4 ounce anisette
- 3/4 ounce light rum
- 1 dash Angostura bitters

Mix the ingredients together, with ice, in the mixing glass and strain into the cocktail glass.

LENA

MEDIUM-DRY APERITIF

- Cocktail glass
- Mixing glass
- 1 ounce bourbon
- 1/2 ounce sweet red vermouth
- 2 tsp. Galliano
- 2 tsp. Campari
- 2 tsp. dry vermouth

GARNISH
- 1 maraschino cherry

Stir all the ingredients together, with ice, in the mixing glass and strain into the chilled cocktail glass. Add the maraschino cherry to the glass.

BRAINSTORM

- Cocktail glass
- Mixing glass
- 1 3/4 ounces Irish whiskey
- 2 dashes Benedictine
- 2 dashes dry vermouth
- Extra: 1 piece of orange peel

DELICATE, DRY DRINK FOR THE EVENING

Stir all the ingredients together, with ice, in the mixing glass and strain into the cocktail glass. Squeeze the orange peel over the drink and add it to the glass.

OPENING

- Cocktail glass
- Shaker
- 1 1/2 ounces bourbon
- 3/4 ounce sweet red vermouth
- 2 tsp. grenadine

SWEET, SHORT DRINK FOR THE EVENING

Shake all the ingredients together, with ice, in the shaker and strain into the cocktail glass.

DREAM OF NAPLES

- Cocktail glass
- Mixing glass
- 1 ounce bourbon
- 2 tsp. Campari
- 2 tsp. triple sec
- 1 dash Angostura bitters
GARNISH
- 1 maraschino cherry

DRY, SPICY DRINK FOR THE EVENING

Stir all the ingredients together, with ice, in the mixing glass and strain into the cocktail glass. Perch the cherry on the rim of the glass.

WHISKEY

BOURBON MINT JULEP

- Goblet
- Mixing glass
- 2 ounces bourbon
- 4 sprigs mint
- 4 tsp. sugar
- 1 dash dark rum or brandy

GARNISH
- 1 slice of lemon (optional)
- 1 sprig of mint

REFRESHING COOLER FOR HOT DAYS

Mix bourbon, 4 sprigs of mint, and sugar in the mixing glass. Pour into the glass with ice cubes and stir until outside of the glass becomes frosted. Top with a dash of dark rum or brandy. Garnish with remaining sprig of mint and slice of lemon. Serve with straws.

SWEET LADY

- Cocktail glass
- Shaker
- 1 1/2 ounces scotch
- 2 tsp. white crème de cacao
- 2 tsp. peach brandy

A FRUITY, MILD DRINK FOR ANY TIME OF THE YEAR

Shake all the ingredients together, with ice, in the shaker and strain into the cocktail glass.

TORONTO

- Cocktail glass
- Shaker
- 2 ounces Canadian whiskey
- 3/4 ounce Fernet Branca or other herbal bitters
- 1 tsp. sugar syrup
- 1 dash Angostura bitters

DELICATE, DRY AFTER-DINNER DRINK

Shake all the ingredients together, with ice, in the shaker and strain into the glass.

Bourbon Mint Julep

WHISKEY

EXPLORATION

FRUITY, DELICATE DRY DRINK FOR THE EVENING

- Rocks glass
- Shaker
- 1 ounce scotch
- 3/4 ounce dry sherry
- 2 tsp. amaretto
- 2 tsp. lemon juice
- Extra: 1 piece of lemon peel

Shake all the ingredients together, with ice, in the shaker and strain into the glass. Squeeze the lemon peel over the drink and add it to the glass.

GLOOM LIFTER

SHARP, FRUITY DRINK FOR THE EVENING

- Cocktail glass
- Shaker
- 1 ounce Irish whiskey
- 2 tsp. lemon juice
- 2 tsp. sugar syrup
- 1 dash of egg white

GARNISH
- 1 slice of lemon

Shake all the ingredients together firmly, with ice, in the shaker and strain into the cocktail glass. Perch the slice of lemon on the rim of the glass.

NIGHT SHADOWS

FRUITY, DELICATELY DRY DRINK FOR THE EVENING

- Rocks glass
- Shaker
- 1 ounce bourbon
- 2 tsp. sweet red vermouth
- 2 tsp. orange juice
- 1 tsp. yellow Chartreuse

GARNISH
- 1/2 slice of orange
- 1 lemon wedge

Shake all the ingredients together, with ice, in the shaker and strain into the glass filled one-third full with crushed ice. Add the fruit to the glass.

YANKEE DUTCH

- Cocktail glass
- Mixing glass
- 1/2 ounce bourbon
- 1/2 ounce cherry brandy
- 1/2 ounce triple sec
- 1/2 ounce vodka
- Extra: 1 piece of orange peel

STRONG DRINK FOR PARTIES

Stir all the ingredients together, with ice, in the mixing glass and strain into the cocktail glass. Squeeze the orange peel over the drink and add it to the glass.

DE RIGUEUR

- Cocktail glass
- Shaker
- 1 1/2 ounces bourbon
- 1 1/2 ounces grapefruit juice
- 2 tsp. honey

FRUITY, DRY DRINK FOR THE EVENING

Shake all the ingredients together firmly, with ice, in the shaker and strain into the cocktail glass.

FRISCO SOUR

- Sour glass
- Shaker
- 1 1/2 ounces bourbon
- 3/4 ounce Benedictine
- 1 ounce lemon juice

SPICY, SOUR AFTER-DRINK DRINK

Shake all the ingredients together, with ice cubes, in the shaker and strain into the glass.

WHISKEY

ALABAMA SLAMMER

- Old-fashioned glass
- Shaker
- 1 ounce whiskey
- 1 ounce sloe gin
- 1 ounce triple sec
- 1 ounce Galliano
- 1 ounce orange juice

GARNISH
- 1 maraschino cherry
- 1 slice of orange

STRONG DRINK FOR PARTIES

Shake the ingredients with cracked ice, strain and pour into the old-fashioned glass. Top up with orange juice.

HURRICANE

- Cocktail glass
- Mixing glass
- 3/4 ounce bourbon
- 3/4 ounce gin
- 3/4 ounce peppermint-flavored liqueur

DELICATE, DRY DRINK FOR THE EVENING

Stir all the ingredients together, with ice, in the mixing glass and strain into the glass.

OLD PAL

- Cocktail glass
- Mixing glass
- 3/4 ounce bourbon
- 3/4 ounce Campari
- 3/4 ounce dry vermouth

SPICY, BITTER APERITIF

Stir all the ingredients together, with ice, in the mixing glass and strain into the glass.

Alabama Slammer

WHISKEY

UP TO DATE

- Cocktail glass
- Mixing glass
- 1 ounce Canadian whiskey
- 3/4 ounce dry vermouth
- 2 tsp. Grand Marnier
- 1 dash Angostura bitters
- Extra: 1 piece of lemon peel (optional)

MEDIUM-DRY APERITIF

Stir the ingredients together, with ice, in the mixing glass and strain into the glass. Squeeze the lemon peel over the cocktail, if liked.

MODERN GIRL

- Rocks glass
- Shaker
- 3/4 ounce bourbon
- 2 tsp. lemon juice
- 1 tsp. light rum
- 1 tsp. Pernod
- 1 tsp. orange bitters
- Extra: 1 piece of lemon peel

SPICY, DRY DRINK FOR THE EVENING

Shake all the ingredients together, with ice, in the shaker and strain into the glass over ice cubes. Squeeze the lemon peel over the drink and add it to the glass.

McKINLEY'S DELIGHT

- Cocktail glass
- Mixing glass
- 1 ounce bourbon
- 1 ounce dry vermouth
- 2 tsp. cherry-flavored liqueur
- 1 tsp. Pernod
GARNISH
1 maraschino cherry

FRUITY, DRY DRINK FOR THE EVENING

Stir all the ingredients together, with ice, in the mixing glass and strain into the cocktail glass. Perch the cherry on the rim of the glass.

LONDON SOUR

- Highball/Collins glass
- Shaker
- 1 ounce scotch
- 3/4 ounce lemon juice
- 3/4 ounce orange juice
- 2 tsp. almond syrup
- 2 tsp. sugar syrup

GARNISH
- 1/2 slice of orange
- 1 maraschino cherry

FRUITY DRINK FOR ANY OCCASION

Shake all the ingredients together, with ice, in the shaker and strain into the glass. Spear the slice of orange and cherry on a toothpick and lay the garnish across the rim of the glass.

MINT COOLER

- Highball/Collins glass
- 1 1/2 ounces scotch
- 1 tsp. white or green crème de menthe
- Sparkling mineral water for topping up

REFRESHING COOLER FOR HOT DAYS

Put the whiskey and crème de menthe in the glass with ice cubes and top up with mineral water. Serve with a stirrer.

CANADIAN SUMMER

- Large rocks glass
- 1 ounce Canadian whiskey
- 3/4 ounce white crème de cacao
- 2 tsp. green crème de menthe
- Soda water for topping up

FRESH, SPICY LONG DRINK FOR ANY TIME OF YEAR

Stir the whiskey and liqueurs together in the glass. Add a few ice cubes and top up with soda water.

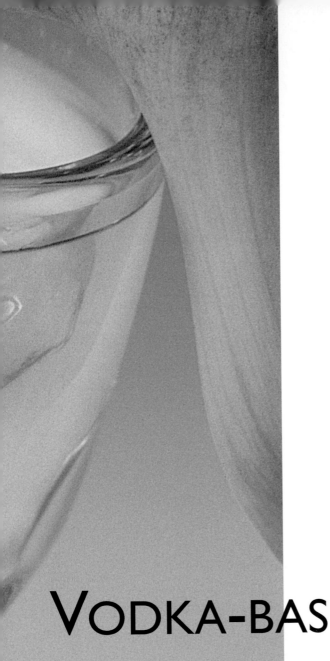

VODKA-BASED DRINKS

VODKA

VODKATINI

- Cocktail glass
- Mixing glass
- 1 1/2 ounces vodka
- 3/4 ounce dry vermouth
- Extra: 1 olive

DRY DRINK FOR A PARTY

Mix the ingredients together, with ice, in the mixing glass and strain into the cocktail glass. Spear the olive on a toothpick and add it to the glass.

OVIDIO

- Champagne glass
- Shaker
- 1 ounce vodka
- 3/4 ounce blue curaçao
- 3/4 ounce grapefruit juice
- Dry champagne or sparkling wine for topping up

GARNISH
- 1/2 slice of lemon
- 1 mint leaf

REFRESHING, DRY CHAMPAGNE COCKTAIL FOR A PARTY

Shake all the ingredients, except the champagne, together, with ice, in the shaker. Strain into the cocktail glass and top up with champagne. Perch the slice of lemon on the rim of the glass and place the mint leaf on top of the drink.

MARAWOD

- Cocktail glass
- Mixing glass
- 1 ounce vodka
- 2 tsp. cherry eau-de-vie
- 2 tsp. maraschino

GARNISH
- 1 maraschino cherry

FRUITY, DELICATE, SWEET DRINK FOR THE EVENING

Mix all the ingredients together, with ice, in the mixing glass and strain into the glass. Spear the cherry on a toothpick and add it to the glass.

Vodka Sidecar

- Cocktail glass
- Shaker
- 3/4 ounce vodka
- 3/4 ounce triple sec
- 1 tsp. lemon juice

BITTERSWEET DRINK FOR THE EVENING

Shake all the ingredients together, with ice, in the shaker and strain into the cocktail glass.

Kangaroo

- Cocktail glass
- Mixing glass
- 1 1/2 ounces vodka
- 3/4 ounce dry vermouth
- Extra: 1 piece of lemon peel

MEDIUM-DRY APERITIF

Mix the ingredients together, with ice, in the mixing glass and strain into the cocktail glass. Squeeze the lemon peel over the drink and add the peel to the glass.

Vodka Alexander

- Cocktail glass
- Shaker
- 1 ounce vodka
- 1/2 ounce white crème de cacao
- 1/2 ounce light cream

GARNISH
- Unsweetened cocoa powder

PIQUANT, SWEET AFTER-DINNER DRINK

Shake all the ingredients together, with ice, in the shaker and strain into the glass. Dust the drink with cocoa powder.

VODKA

MARK ONE

SPICY, SHORT DRINK

- Cocktail glass
- Mixing glass
- 1/2 ounce vodka
- 1/2 ounce green Chartreuse
- 1/2 ounce Cinzano

Pour the ingredients into a mixing glass with ice cubes. Stir and strain into the cocktail glass.

PACIFIC BLUE

SWEET DRINK FOR A PARTY

- Cocktail glass with a sugared rim
- Mixing glass
- 3/4 ounce crème de banane
- 3/4 ounce blue curaçao
- 2 tsp. vodka
- 2 tsp. coconut-flavored liqueur

GARNISH
- 1 maraschino cherry

Mix the ingredients together, with ice, in the mixing glass and strain into the glass with the sugared rim. Perch the cherry on the rim of the glass.

AMATO

FRUITY, DELICATE, DRY DRINK FOR THE EVENING

- Large cocktail glass
- Mixing glass
- 3/4 ounce vodka
- 3/4 ounce dry vermouth
- 3/4 ounce mandarin-flavored liqueur
- Extra: 1 piece of orange peel

Mix all the ingredients together, with ice, in the mixing glass and strain into the glass over ice cubes. Squeeze the orange peel over the drink and add the peel to the glass.

Mark One

VODKA

VODKA GIMLET

MEDIUM-DRY APERITIF

- Cocktail glass
- Mixing glass
- 1 1/2 ounces vodka
- 3/4 ounce lime juice
- Extra: 1/2 slice of lime

Mix the ingredients together, with ice, in the mixing glass and strain into the glass. Add the slice of lime to the glass.

RED SQUARE

PIQUANT, DELICATE, DRY DRINK FOR ANY TIME OF YEAR

- Cocktail glass
- Shaker
- 3/4 ounce vodka
- 3/4 ounce white crème de cacao
- 2 tsp. lemon juice
- 1 1/2 tsp. grenadine
GARNISH
- 1 maraschino cherry

Shake all the ingredients together firmly, with ice, in the shaker and strain into the glass. Perch the cherry on the rim of the glass.

IVAN COLLINS

REFRESHING DRINK FOR ANY TIME OF THE DAY

- Collins/highball glass
- 1 1/2 ounces vodka
- 3/4 ounce lemon juice
- 2 tsp. sugar syrup
- Soda water for topping up
GARNISH
- 1/2 slice of lemon
- 1 green maraschino cherry

Put all the ingredients, except the soda water, in the Collins glass with ice cubes, top up with soda water, and stir well. Perch the slice of lemon on the rim of the glass and add the cherry to the glass. Serve with a long stirrer.

WHITE RUSSIAN

- Cocktail glass
- Mixing glass
- 1 ounce vodka
- 3/4 ounce coffee-flavored liqueur
- 2 tsp. light cream

CREAMY DRINK FOR ANY TIME OF THE DAY

Mix the vodka and liqueur together, with ice, in the mixing glass and strain into the cocktail glass. Lightly whip the cream and put it on top of the drink. This cocktail can also be drunk with ice cubes; if you do, serve it in a rocks glass.

FESTRUS

- Cocktail glass
- Mixing glass
- 3/4 ounce vodka
- 3/4 ounce Grand Marnier
- 3/4 ounce Cinzano
- Extra: 1 piece of orange peel

MEDIUM-DRY APERITIF

Mix the ingredients together, with ice, in the mixing glass and strain into the cocktail glass. Squeeze the orange peel over the drink and add it to the glass.

FLYING GRASSHOPPER

- Cocktail glass
- Mixing glass
- 3/4 ounce vodka
- 2 tsp. white crème de cacao
- 2 tsp. green crème de menthe
GARNISH
- 1 green maraschino cherry

SPICY, SWEET DRINK FOR THE EVENING

Mix the ingredients together, with ice, in the mixing glass and strain into the glass. Perch the cherry on the rim of the glass.

VODKA

BLOODSHOT

SPICY TASTY DRINK

- Highball/Collins glass
- Shaker
- 2 ounces vodka
- 2 ounces beef bouillon
- 2½ ounces tomato juice
- 1 dash lime juice
- 1 dash Worcestershire sauce
- 1 dash Tabasco sauce
- Black pepper
- Celery salt

GARNISH
- 2 lime slices
- 2 cherry tomatoes

Shake the ingredients together in a shaker, with ice. Strain into a highball glass half-filled with ice and garnish with the fruit.

TRIPLE SUN

AROMATIC DRINK FOR A PARTY

- Cocktail glass
- Mixing glass
- ½ ounce vodka
- ½ ounce banana-flavored liqueur
- ½ ounce sweet white vermouth
- ½ ounce dry vermouth
- 2 dashes grenadine

GARNISH
- 1 maraschino cherry

Mix the ingredients together, with ice, in the mixing glass and strain into the cocktail glass. Add the cherry to the glass.

RUSSIAN NIGHT

DELICATELY PIQUANT, MILD DRINK FOR THE EVENING

- Cocktail glass
- Shaker
- 1½ ounces vodka
- 2 tsp. blue curaçao
- 1 dash Pernod

GARNISH
- 1 maraschino cherry

Shake all the ingredients together, with ice, in the shaker and strain into the glass. Spear the maraschino cherry on a toothpick and add it to the glass.

Bloodshot

VODKA

TRIP

DRY APERITIF

- Cocktail glass
- Mixing glass
- 3/4 ounce vodka
- 3/4 ounce lime cordial
- 3/4 ounce Noilly Prat or other dry vermouth
- Extra: 1 piece of lime peel

Mix the ingredients together, with ice, in the mixing glass and strain into cocktail glass. Squeeze the lime peel over the drink and add the peel to the glass.

GOLDFINGER

FRUITY, DELICATELY PIQUANT DRINK FOR THE EVENING

- Cocktail glass
- Shaker
- 1 1/2 ounces Cinzano (rosso antico)
- 3/4 ounce vodka
- 2 tsp. orange juice
- 1 dash orange bitters

Shake all the ingredients together, with ice, in the shaker and strain into the glass.

GRAND DUCHESSE

BITTERSWEET DRINK FOR THE EVENING

- Champagne or cocktail glass
- Shaker
- 1 ounce vodka
- 2 tsp. light rum
- 2 tsp. lemon juice
- 1 tsp. grenadine

Shake all the ingredients together, with ice, in the shaker and strain into the glass.

WHITE CAP

- Cocktail glass
- Shaker
- 1 ounce vodka
- 2 tsp. mocha-flavored liqueur
- 2 tsp. port
- 2 tsp. lightly whipped cream

CREAMY DRINK FOR THE AFTERNOON

Shake all the ingredients, except the cream, together, with ice, in the shaker and strain into the cocktail glass. Top the drink with the cream.

ROULETTE

- Highball/Collins glass
- 1 ounce vodka
- 1 ounce Campari
- 1 ounce orange juice
- 2 tsp. grenadine
- Extra: 1/2 slice of orange

FRUITY, BITTER AFTER-DINNER DRINK

Mix the ingredients together, with ice, in the highball glass. Add the slice of orange to the glass. Serve with a stirrer.

BALTIC

- Highball/Collins glass
- 1 ounce plus 1 tsp. vodka
- 1 tsp. blue curaçao
- 1/2 ounce passion-fruit juice
- 1 tsp. lemon juice
- Orange juice for topping up
GARNISH
- 1/2 slice orange
- 1 maraschino cherry

FRUITY DRINK FOR THE SUMMER

Stir all the ingredients together, with ice cubes, in the highball glass. Spear the slice of orange and cherry on a toothpick, and perch the garnish on the rim of the glass.

VODKA

HARVEY WALLBANGER

FRUITY APERITIF OR AFTER-DINNER DRINK

- Highball/Collins glass
- 1 ounce vodka
- Orange juice for topping up
- 2 tsp. Galliano

GARNISH
- 1/2 slice of orange (optional)

Pour the vodka into the glass over ice cubes. Top up with orange juice, stir the drink, and pour the Galliano on top. Perch the slice of orange on the rim of the glass. Serve with a stirrer.

BLUE AEGEAN

FRUITY DRINK FOR THE SUMMER

- Highball/Collins glass
- 3/4 ounce vodka
- 3/4 ounce blue curaçao
- 3/4 ounce Grand Marnier
- Mixture of pineapple and lemon juices for topping up

GARNISH
- 1/2 slice of pineapple
- 1 maraschino cherry
- Sprig of mint

Mix the spirits together thoroughly, with ice cubes, in the highball glass and top up with the mixture of juices. Spear the slice of pineapple, cherry and sprig of mint on a toothpick and perch the garnish on the rim of the glass.

NORDIC SUMMER

FRUITY, DELICATE, DRY DRINK FOR A PARTY

- Highball/collins glass
- 2 3/4 ounces orange juice
- 1 1/2 ounces vodka
- 3/4 ounce passion-fruit syrup
- 3/4 ounce lime juice
- 1 dash grenadine (optional)

GARNISH
- 1 slice of lime
- 1 maraschino cherry

Carefully stir all the ingredients together, with ice, in the highball glass. Perch the fruit on the rim of the glass.

Harvey Wallbanger

VODKA

MANBOLS

- Highball/Collins glass
- 1 1/2 ounces mandarin-flavored liqueur
- 3/4 ounce vodka
- 3/4 ounce lemon juice
- 2 tsp. grenadine
- Tonic water for topping up

GARNISH
- 1 slice of mandarin orange
- 1 slice of lemon
- 1 maraschino cherry

FRUITY DRINK FOR HOT DAYS

Stir the ingredients together, with ice cubes, in the highball glass. Spear the slice of mandarin orange, lemon and cherry on a toothpick and lay the garnish across the rim of the glass. Serve with a stirrer.

SIMINEN RAKKAUS

- Cocktail glass
- Shaker
- 3/4 ounce vodka
- 3/4 ounce crème de banane
- 2 tsp. Parfait Amour
- 2 tsp. lemon juice

GARNISH
- 1 maraschino cherry

FRUITY DRINK FOR A PARTY

Shake all the ingredients together, with ice, in the shaker and strain into the glass. Spear the cherry on a toothpick and add it to the glass.

BABYFACE

- Champagne or cocktail glass
- Shaker
- 3/4 ounce vodka
- 3/4 ounce light cream
- 3/4 ounce crème de cassis

FRUITY, SWEET AFTER-DINNER DRINK

Shake all the ingredients together firmly, with ice, in the shaker and strain into the glass.

SONIA

SPICY AFTER-DINNER DRINK

- Champagne or cocktail glass
- Shaker
- 1 ounce vodka
- 1 ounce green peppermint-flavored liqueur

GARNISH
- 1 sprig of mint

Shake all the ingredients together, with ice, in the shaker and strain into the glass. Perch the sprig of mint on the rim of the glass.

LOVER'S NOCTURNE

DELICATE, DRY AFTER-DINNER DRINK

- Cocktail glass
- Mixing glass
- 1 1/2 ounces vodka
- 2 tsp. Drambuie
- 1 dash Angostura bitters

Mix all the ingredients together, with ice, in the mixing glass and strain into the cocktail glass.

PLAZA

REFRESHING DRINK FOR THE SUMMER

- Highball/Collins glass
- 1 1/2 ounces vodka
- 3/4 ounce passion-fruit flavored liqueur
- 3/4 ounce cream of coconut
- Soda water for topping up

GARNISH
- 1 slice of orange
- 1 maraschino cherry

Carefully mix the ingredients together, with ice cubes, in the highball glass. Perch the slice of orange on the rim of the glass and fasten the cherry to it with a toothpick. Put a stirrer in the glass and serve the drink immediately.

VODKA

SLOE DANCE

- Highball/Collins glass
- Mixing glass
- 1 ounce vodka
- 1/2 ounce Southern Comfort
- 1/2 ounce sloe gin
- Orange juice for topping up

GARNISH
- 1 piece of orange peel spiral

REFRESHING, FRUITY DRINK

Pour the ingredients, except the orange juice, into a mixing glass and stir. Pour drinks into the highball glass, half-filled with ice cubes. Top up with fresh orange juice. Garnish with the orange peel.

SERRERA

- Highball/Collins glass
- Shaker
- 1 ounce vodka
- 3/4 ounce blue curaçao
- 2 tsp. lemon juice
- Soda water for topping up

GARNISH
- 1/4 slice of pineapple
- 1 piece of orange peel
- 1 maraschino cherry

REFRESHING DRINK FOR THE SUMMER

Shake all the ingredients together, except the soda water, with ice, in the shaker. Strain into the highball glass over ice cubes, and top up with soda water. Spear the slice of pineapple, orange peel, and cherry on a toothpick and perch the garnish on the rim of the glass. Serve with a stirrer.

CONSUL

- Highball/Collins glass
- Shaker
- 1 1/2 ounces grapefruit juice
- 1 ounce vodka
- 3/4 ounce raspberry-flavored liqueur
- 2 tsp. lemon juice

DRY, FRUITY DRINK FOR A PARTY

Shake the ingredients together, with ice, in the shaker and strain into the highball glass over ice cubes.

Sloe Dance

VODKA

SWINGER

BITTERSWEET DRINK FOR A PARTY

- Highball/Collins glass
- Shaker
- 2³/4 ounces orange juice
- 1¹/2 ounces vodka
- ³/4 ounce amaretto
- 2 tsp. lime juice

GARNISH

- 1 slice of orange

Shake all the ingredients together, firmly, with ice cubes, in the shaker and strain into the highball glass. Perch the slice of orange on the rim of the glass.

VODKA SOUR

REFRESHING DRINK FOR A PARTY

- Rocks glass
- Shaker
- 1¹/2 ounces vodka
- ³/4 ounce lemon juice
- 2 tsp. sugar syrup
- Extra: ¹/2 slice of lemon and maraschino cherry

Shake all the ingredients together, with ice, in the shaker and strain into the glass. Add the fruit to the glass. Add a little mineral water too, if liked.

NIKKO

FRUITY DRINK FOR THE SUMMER

- Highball/Collins glass
- Shaker
- 1 ounce plus 1 tsp. vodka
- ¹/2 ounce blue curaçao
- 1 tsp. lemon juice
- 1 tsp. pineapple juice
- Orange juice for topping up

GARNISH

- 1 sprig of mint

Shake all the ingredients, except the orange juice, together, with ice, in the shaker. Strain into the glass over ice cubes, top up with the orange juice and stir. Add the sprig of mint and add a stirrer to the glass.

CASABLANCA

FRUITY, CREAMY DRINK FOR THE EVENING

- Highball/Collins glass
- Shaker
- 1 1/2 ounces orange juice
- 1 ounce vodka
- 3/4 ounce advocaat
- 3/4 ounce lemon juice

Shake all the ingredients together well, with ice cubes, in the shaker. Half fill the highball glass with crushed ice and strain the cocktail glass.

LE MANS

DELICATE, DRY DRINK FOR A PARTY

- Large rocks glass
- 1 ounce vodka
- 1 ounce Cointreau or other orange-flavored liqueur
- Soda water for topping up

GARNISH
- 1 slice of lemon

Mix the vodka and Cointreau together, with ice cubes, in the glass. Top up the soda water and stir briefly. Perch the slice of lemon on the rim of the glass.

CAMURAI

CREAMY DRINK FOR THE SUMMER

- Highball/Collins glass
- 1 ounce vodka
- 1/2 ounce blue curaçao
- 1/2 ounce cream of coconut
- Soda water for topping up

GARNISH
- 1 maraschino cherry
- 1 piece of orange peel
- 1 piece of lemon peel

Carefully mix the ingredients together in the highball glass. Spear the cherry and slices of citrus fruit on a toothpick and lay the garnish across the rim of the glass. Serve with a stirrer.

VODKA

BLUE LAGOON

FRUITY, SWEET DRINK FOR SUMMER

- Highball/Collins glass
- 1 1/2 ounces vodka
- 3/4 ounce blue curaçao
- 1 tsp. lemon juice
- Lemonade for topping up

GARNISH
- 1 slice of lemon (or 3 maraschino cherries)

Mix the ingredients, except the lemonade, together, with ice cubes, in the highball glass. Top up with lemonade and stir briefly. Perch the slice of lemon on the rim of the glass. If using maraschino cherries, spear them with a toothpick and rest them on top of the glass.

APRICOT DAILY

DRY, FRUITY DRINK FOR THE EVENING

- Highball/Collins glass
- Shaker
- 1 1/2 ounces vodka
- 3/4 ounce apricot brandy
- 2 tsp. lemon juice
- Bitter lemon for topping up

Shake all the ingredients, except the bitter lemon, together, with ice, in the shaker and strain into the glass. Top up with bitter lemon and stir briefly.

GREEN PEACE

SWEET DRINK FOR THE SUMMER

- Highball/Collins glass
- 1/2 ounce vodka
- 1/2 ounce dry vermouth
- 1/2 ounce Pisang Ambon
- 2 tsp. apricot brandy
- Pineapple juice for topping up

GARNISH
- 1 maraschino cherry

Stir the ingredients together, with crushed ice or ice cubes, in the highball glass. Perch the cherry on the rim of the glass. Serve with a stirrer.

Blue Lagoon

VODKA

GREEN SPIDER

SPICY, FRESH DRINK FOR THE SUMMER

- Highball/Collins glass
- 1 1/2 ounces vodka
- 3/4 ounce peppermint cordial
- Soda water for topping up

GARNISH
- 1 sprig of mint

Mix the vodka and cordial together, with ice, in the glass. Top up with the soda water and stir briefly. Perch the sprig of mint on the rim of the glass.

HAPPY FIN

FRUITY, REFRESHING DRINK FOR THE SUMMER

- Highball/Collins glass
- 1 1/2 ounces vodka
- 3/4 ounce peach-flavored liqueur
- Orange juice for topping up

GARNISH
- 1/2 slice of orange
- 1 maraschino cherry

Mix the ingredients together, with ice cubes, in the highball glass. Spear the slice of orange and maraschino cherry on a toothpick and perch the garnish on the rim of the glass.

BITTERSWEET

FRUITY, DELICATE, DRY DRINK FOR THE SUMMER

- Highball/Collins glass
- 1 large scoop lemon sorbet
- 3/4 ounce vodka
- 3/4 ounce grapefruit juice
- 3/4 ounce lemon cordial
- Soda water for topping up

Mix together the scoop of sorbet, vodka, grapefruit juice, and lemon cordial in the highball glass. Top up the soda water and stir briefly. Serve with a spoon.

FOLK BOAT

- Highball/Collins glass
- Shaker
- 2 ounces pineapple juice
- 1 1/2 ounces vodka
- 3/4 ounce blue curaçao
- 2 tsp. passion-fruit syrup
- 1 dash lime juice

GARNISH
- 1/2 slice of orange
- 1 green maraschino cherry

FRUITY DRINK FOR THE SUMMER

Shake the ingredients together, with ice, in the shaker and strain into the highball glass. Perch the slice of orange and the cherry on the rim of the glass.

INDIANAPOLIS

- Cocktail glass
- Shaker
- 3/4 ounce vodka
- 3/4 ounce blue curaçao
- 3/4 ounce light cream

CREAMY DRINK FOR THE EVENING

Shake the ingredients together firmly, with ice, in the shaker and strain into the cocktail glass.

VOLGA CLIPPER

- Cocktail glass
- Shaker
- 1 ounce vodka
- 1 ounce orange juice
- 3/4 ounce apricot brandy

FRUITY, SWEET DRINK FOR THE EVENING

Shake the ingredients together, with ice, in the shaker and strain into the cocktail glass.

VODKA

JUSTINE

- Martini glass
- Shaker
- 2 ounces vodka
- 1 ounce crème de noyau
- 1 ounce kirsch
- 2–3 dashes of orgeat syrup or amaretto
- Whipping cream

STRONG, AROMATIC DRINK

Shake the ingredients together in the shaker, with ice, and strain into the Martini glass.

AVIATION

- Cocktail glass
- Shaker
- 1 ounce vodka
- 1/2 ounce lemon juice
- 1 tsp. apricot brandy
- 2 dashes maraschino

MEDIUM-DRY APERITIF

Shake the ingredients together, with ice, in the shaker and strain into the cocktail glass.

ROBERTA

- Cocktail glass
- Mixing glass
- 3/4 ounce vodka
- 3/4 ounce dry vermouth
- 3/4 ounce cherry-flavored liqueur
- 2 dashes Campari
- 2 dashes crème de banane
- Extra: 1 piece of orange peel

MEDIUM-DRY APERITIF

Mix the ingredients together, with ice, in the mixing glass and strain into the cocktail glass. Squeeze the orange peel over the drink.

Justine

VODKA

CRISTA SOLAR

PIQUANT DRINK FOR A PARTY

- Cocktail glass
- Mixing glass
- 1 ounce vodka
- 2 tsp. triple sec
- 2 tsp. port
- 2 tsp. dry vermouth
- 2 dashes Angostura bitters
- Extra: 1 pearl onion and 1 piece of orange peel

Mix the ingredients together, with ice, in the mixing glass and strain into the cocktail glass. Squeeze the orange peel over the drink; spear the onion on a toothpick and add it to the glass.

GREEN HOPE

MEDIUM-DRY APERITIF

- Cocktail glass
- Shaker
- 1 ounce vodka
- 1/2 ounce green curaçao
- 2 tsp. crème de banane
- 2 tsp. grape juice
- 2 tsp. lemon juice

GARNISH
- 1 red and 1 green maraschino cherry

Shake the ingredients together, with ice, in the shaker and strain into the cocktail glass. Spear the cherries on a toothpick and lay the garnish across the rim of the glass.

COLONEL KREMLIN

FRUITY, DELICATE, DRY DRINK FOR THE EVENING

- Cocktail glass
- Shaker
- 1 1/2 ounces vodka
- 2 tsp. lime juice
- 2 tsp. sugar syrup
- Extra: 3 mint leaves

Shake the ingredients together firmly, with ice, in the shaker and strain into the glass. Finely chop the mint and add it to the glass.

Finnish Cockbull

Spicy, sweet drink for the evening

- Cocktail glass
- Mixing glass
- 1 ounce vodka
- 3/4 ounce amaretto
- 2 tsp. coffee-flavored liqueur

Garnish
- 1/4 slice of pineapple

Mix all the ingredients together, with ice, in the mixing glass and strain into the cocktail glass. Perch the slice of pineapple on the rim of the glass.

Long Volga Clipper

Fruity, delicate, dry drink for a party

- Highball/Collins glass
- Shaker
- 1 ounce vodka
- 1 ounce orange juice
- 3/4 ounce apricot brandy
- Bitter orange for topping up

Garnish
- 1 kumquat

Shake the vodka, orange juice, and apricot brandy together well, with ice cubes, in the shaker and strain into the highball glass. Top up with bitter orange and stir well. Perch the kumquat on the rim of the glass.

Pedi Cocktail

Piquant aperitif

- Cocktail glass
- Mixing glass
- 1 ounce vodka
- 3/4 ounce Campari
- 2 tsp. triple sec

Garnish
- 1 maraschino cherry
- 1/2 slice of lemon

Mix the ingredients together, with ice, in the mixing glass and strain into the cocktail glass. Spear the slice of lemon and maraschino cherry on a toothpick and lay the garnish across the rim of the glass.

VODKA

MADAM I'M ADAM

- Goblet
- Shaker
- 1 ounce vodka
- 1 dash triple sec
- 1 ounce cranberry juice
- 1 ounce grapefruit juice
- 1/2 ounce pineapple juice

GARNISH
- Lime peel
- 1 strawberry

PIQUANT DRINK FOR A PARTY

Shake the ingredients together, except the pineapple juice, with ice, in a shaker and strain into the glass. Shake the pineapple juice, with cracked ice, until a froth is formed and spoon it over the top.

GALWAY SUNRISE

- Cocktail glass
- Shaker
- 1 ounce Drambuie
- 3/4 ounce orange juice
- 1/2 ounce vodka
- 2 tsp. triple sec
- 1 dash of Frothee

FRUITY DRINK FOR A PARTY

Shake the ingredients together, with ice, in the shaker and strain into the glass.

DAY DREAMER

- Cocktail glass
- Mixing glass
- 1 ounce vodka
- 2 tsp. dry vermouth
- 2 tsp. dry sherry
- Extra: 1 piece of lemon peel

PIQUANT, DRY APERITIF

Mix the ingredients together well, with ice, in the mixing glass and strain into the glass. Squeeze the lemon peel over the drink and add the peel to the glass.

Madam I'm Adam

VODKA

BARBARA

SWEET, CREAMY DRINK

- Cocktail glass
- Shaker
- 3/4 ounce vodka
- 3/4 ounce white crème de cacao
- 3/4 ounce light cream
- Extra: Grated nutmeg

Shake the ingredients together firmly, with ice, in the shaker and strain into the glass. Sprinkle a little grated nutmeg on top.

TARANTELLA

BITTER CHAMPAGNE COCKTAIL FOR A RECEPTION

- Champagne glass or flute
- Mixing glass
- 1/2 ounce vodka
- 1/2 ounce triple sec
- 1/2 ounce Campari
- Dry champagne or sparkling wine for topping up

GARNISH
- 1 piece of pineapple
- 1 maraschino cherry

Mix all the ingredients, except the champagne, together, with ice, in the mixing glass. Strain into the champagne glass and top up with champagne. Perch the piece of pineapple on the rim of the glass and fasten the maraschino cherry to it with a toothpick.

RUSSIAN CAR

CREAMY, SWEET AFTER-DINNER DRINK

- Large cocktail glass
- Shaker
- 1 1/2 ounces vodka
- 1 1/2 ounces light cream
- 2 tsp. Galliano
- 2 tsp. white crème de cacao

Shake all the ingredients together, with ice, in the shaker and strain into the glass.

MONTE ROSA

LIGHT, SHORT APERITIF

- Cocktail glass
- Shaker
- 3/4 ounce vodka
- 2 tsp. triple sec
- 2 tsp. Campari
- 2 tsp. orange juice

Shake the ingredients together, with ice, in the shaker and strain into the cocktail glass.

VODKA NIKOLASCHKA

MILD, FRUITY DRINK FOR A PARTY

- Shot glass
- 3/4 ounce vodka
- 1 slice of orange, peeled
- 1 tsp. sugar
- 1 dash Grand Marnier

Pour the vodka into the glass. Place the slice of orange on top of the glass, sprinkle the sugar on top and drizzle with Grand Marnier. You are supposed to eat the orange and drink the vodka at the same time.

EAST WIND

SPICY, DELICATE, DRY APERITIF

- Cocktail glass
- Mixing glass
- 3/4 ounce vodka
- 3/4 ounce dry vermouth
- 3/4 ounce sweet red vermouth
GARNISH
- 1/2 slice of orange
- 1/2 slice of lemon

Stir all the ingredients together, with ice cubes, in the cocktail glass. Perch the slices of fruit on the rim of the glass.

VODKA

BLACK RUSSIAN

- Cocktail glass
- Mixing glass
- 1 1/2 ounces vodka
- 3/4 ounce coffee-flavored liqueur

SWEET, SHORT DRINK FOR THE EVENING

Mix the ingredients together, with ice, in the mixing glass and strain into the cocktail glass.

FINLANDIA

- Cocktail glass
- Shaker
- 1 ounce vodka
- 1 ounce Southern Comfort
- 3/4 ounce light cream
- 1 dash lemon juice
- Extra: Grated nutmeg

PIQUANT, SWEET AFTER-DINNER DRINK

Shake all the ingredients together, with ice, in the shaker and strain into the glass. Sprinkle with grated nutmeg.

FREEDOM

- Cocktail glass
- Shaker
- 3/4 ounce vodka
- 2 tsp. triple sec
- 2 tsp. crème de cassis
- 2 tsp. lemon juice
- Extra: 1 piece of lemon peel

FRUITY, ELEGANT, DRY DRINK FOR ANY TIME OF THE YEAR

Shake the ingredients together well, with ice, in the shaker and strain into the glass. Squeeze the lemon peel over the drink and add the peel to the glass.

Black Russian

VODKA

VODKA AND PEPPERMINT

- Highball/Collins glass
- Shaker
- 3/4 ounce vodka
- 3/4 ounce peppermint cordial
- Tonic water for topping up

GARNISH
- 1 lemon peel spiral

DRY, SPICY DRINK FOR A PARTY

Shake the vodka and cordial together, with ice, in the shaker and strain into the glass. Top up with the tonic and stir briefly. Hang the lemon peel spiral over the rim of the glass.

RED DREAMS

- Cocktail glass
- Shaker
- 1 ounce vodka
- 2 tsp. cherry-flavored liqueur
- 2 tsp. lime juice

GARNISH
- 1 maraschino cherry

FRUITY, DELICATE, DRY DRINK FOR THE EVENING

Shake the ingredients together, with ice, in the shaker and strain into the glass. Perch the cherry on the rim of the glass.

E.P.U.

- Sherry glass
- 1 egg yolk
- Freshly ground black pepper
- Salt
- Hot-pepper sauce
- 3/4 ounce vodka
- 3/4 ounce Sangrita

SPICY, PIQUANT PICK-ME-UP

Put the egg yolk into the sherry glass. Add the seasonings, vodka, and Sangrita. The drink should be tossed back and consumed in one swallow.

PEACH BUCK

SWEET, REFRESHING LONG DRINK

- Highball/Collins glass
- Shaker
- 2 ounces vodka
- 1 ounce peach brandy
- 1 ounce lemon juice
- Ginger ale for topping up

GARNISH
- 1 peach slice

Combine all the ingredients, except the ginger ale, with cracked ice in a shaker. Shake and pour into the glass. Top up with ginger ale and stir gently. Garnish with fruit.

RUSSIAN BEAR

SHORT, BITTER DRINK

- Cocktail glass
- Shaker
- 2 ounces vodka
- 1 ounce dark crème de cacao
- 1/2 ounce half-and-half

Shake all the ingredients, with ice, in a shaker and strain into a cocktail glass.

SEX ON THE BEACH

LONG, FRUITY DRINK FOR THE DAYTIME

- Highball/Collins glass
- 2 ounces vodka
- 1 1/2 ounces peach schnapps
- 3 ounces cranberry juice
- 3 ounces pineapple juice

GARNISH
- 1 maraschino cherry

Pour all the ingredients, half-filled with ice cubes, into the highball glass and stir well. Garnish with cherry.

VODKA

BEHIND THE WALL

- Rocks glass
- 1 ounce orange juice
- 1 ounce vodka
- 1/2 ounce mandarin-flavored liqueur
- 1/2 ounce Galliano
- Ginger ale for topping up

GARNISH
- 1/2 slice of orange

FRUITY, REFRESHING DRINK

Shake all the ingredients, except the ginger ale, with ice, in a shaker and strain into glass. Top up with ginger ale. Garnish with orange.

SHARK ATTACK

- Highball/Collins glass
- 3 ounces vodka
- 1 1/2 ounces lemonade
- 2 dashes grenadine

SWEET, REFRESHING SUMMER DRINK

In a Collins glass over ice cubes, pour in the ingredients and stir well.

SOVIET

- Old-fashioned glass
- Shaker
- 3 ounces vodka
- 1 ounce sherry
- 1/2 ounce dry vermouth

GARNISH
- 1 piece of lemon peel

DRY DRINK FOR THE EVENING

Shake all the ingredients, with ice, in a shaker and pour into old-fashioned glass over ice cubes. Garnish with lemon.

Behind the Wall

VODKA

SCREWDRIVER

FRUITY APERITIF OR AFTER-DINNER DRINK

- Rocks glass
- 1 1/2 ounces vodka
- Orange juice for topping up

Garnish
- 1/2 slice of orange

Pour the vodka into the glass, with ice cubes, and top up with orange juice. Perch the slice of orange on the rim of the glass.

FINNISH VIRGIN

FRUITY, BITTERSWEET DRINK FOR THE EVENING

- Cocktail glass
- Shaker
- 1 3/4 ounces vodka
- 1 tsp. orange juice
- 1 tsp. almond syrup
- 1 tsp. lime juice

GARNISH
- 1 maraschino cherry

Shake all the ingredients together, with ice, in the shaker and strain into the glass. Perch the cherry on the rim of the glass.

BALANCE

FRUITY, DELICATE DRY DRINK FOR THE EVENING

- Cocktail glass with sugared rim
- Shaker
- 3/4 ounce vodka
- 2 tsp. light rum
- 2 tsp. triple sec
- 1 tsp. grenadine

GARNISH
- 1 maraschino cherry

Shake all the ingredients together, with ice, in the shaker and strain into the glass with the sugared rim. Spear the cherry with the toothpick and add it to the glass.

VODKA STINGER

SPICY, FRESH DRINK FOR THE EVENING

- Rocks glass
- 1 ounce vodka
- 3/4 ounce green crème de menthe

Stir the ingredients together, with ice cube, in the glass.

BLOODY MARY

SPICY, PIQUANT PICK-ME-UP

- Highball/Collins glass
- 1 3/4 ounces tomato juice
- 1 1/2 ounces vodka
- 2 tsp. lemon juice
- Worcestershire sauce
- Salt
- Freshly ground black pepper
- Hot-pepper sauce
- Celery salt

GARNISH
- 1 small celery stalk (optional)

Mix the ingredients together, with ice cubes, in the highball glass. Add the celery, if liked.

HUNTSMAN

BITTERSWEET DRINK

- Cocktail glass
- Shaker
- 2 ounces vodka
- 1 ounce dark rum
- 1 ounce fresh lime juice
- 1/2 tsp. sugar

Mix the ingredients together in the shaker, with ice. Shake well and strain into the cocktail glass.

VODKA

SERENISSIMA

- Goblet
- Shaker
- 2 ounces vodka
- 2 ounces grapefruit juice
- 1–2 dashes Campari

CALMING, SWEET DRINK

Mix the ingredients together in the shaker, with ice, and shake well. Strain into a goblet half-filled with ice cubes.

ICE PICK

- Highball/Collins glass
- 2 ounces vodka
- Iced tea for topping up
- Extra: Lime wedge

LONG, REFRESHING DRINK FOR THE AFTERNOON

Pour vodka and iced tea into a highball glass filled with ice cubes. Squeeze the lime wedge over drink and drop in. Stir.

JUNGLE JAMES

- Rocks glass
- Blender
- 2 ounces vodka
- 2 ounces crème de bananes
- 2 ounces milk

SMOOTH, SWEET DRINK

Put all ingredients, with ice, in a blender. Blend until smooth and pour into chilled rocks glass.

Serenissima

VODKA

BIKINI

- Cocktail glass
- Shaker
- 3 ounces vodka
- Juice of $1/2$ lemon
- 1 ounce white rum
- $1/2$ ounce milk
- 1 tsp. sugar

SMOOTH, FRUITY DRINK

Pour ingredients into shaker and shake well. Strain into the glass.

GREEN DEMON

- Goblet
- Shaker
- 1 ounce vodka
- 1 ounce light rum
- 1 ounce melon liqueur
- Lemonade for topping up

GARNISH
- 1 piece of watermelon
- 1 maraschino cherry

COLORFUL, FRUITY DRINK

Shake all the ingredients, with ice, in the shaker and pour into the goblet over ice cubes. Fill with lemonade. Garnish with watermelon and cherry. Serve with a straw.

KAMIKAZE

- Cocktail glass
- Shaker
- 3 ounces vodka
- $1/2$ tsp. triple sec
- $1/2$ tsp. fresh lime juice

GARNISH
- 1 lime wedge

FRUITY DRINK FOR A PARTY

Shake all the ingredients, with ice, in a shaker and strain into the cocktail glass. Garnish with lime.

LONG ISLAND ICED TEA

REFRESHING DRINK FOR A PARTY

- Highball/Collins glass
- 2 tsp. vodka
- 2 tsp. gin
- 2 tsp. light rum
- 2 tsp. triple sec
- 2 tsp. white tequila
- 2 tsp. lemon juice
- Cola for topping up

GARNISH
- 1/2 slice of lemon
- 1 sprig of mint

Mix all the ingredients, except the cola, together, with ice, in a highball glass and top up with cola. Perch the slice of lemon and the sprig of mint on the rim of the glass. Serve with a stirrer.

PERFECT LOVE

MILD DRINK FOR THE EVENING

- Highball/Collins glass
- 2 ounces vodka
- 1 ounce parfait amour
- 1 ounce maraschino

Garnish
- 1 twist of lemon peel

Pour the ingredients, in the order listed above, over ice. Garnish with lemon peel.

SALTY DOG

FRUITY APERITIF OR AFTER-DINNER DRINK

- Rocks glass with a salted rim
- 1 1/2 ounces vodka
- Grapefruit juice for topping up

Pour the vodka into the glass with the salted rim and top up with grapefruit juice.

GIN-BASED DRINKS

GIN

WHITE WINGS

TANGY, DRY APERITIF

- Cocktail glass
- Mixing glass
- 1 ounce gin
- $^1/_2$ ounce white crème de menthe

Mix the ingredients together, with ice, in the mixing glass and strain into the cocktail glass.

GIN STINGER

AROMATIC APERITIF OR AFTER-DINNER DRINK

- Cocktail glass
- Mixing glass
- 1 ounce gin
- 1 ounce green crème de menthe

Mix the ingredients together, with ice, in the mixing glass and strain into the cocktail glass.

RED GIN

MEDIUM-DRY APERITIF OR AFTER-DINNER DRINK

- Cocktail glass
- Shaker
- 1$^1/_2$ ounces gin
- 2 tsp. cherry brandy

GARNISH
- 1 slice of orange

Shake the ingredients together well, with ice cubes, in the shaker and strain into the cocktail glass. Perch the slice of orange on the rim of the glass.

QUEBEC

- Cocktail glass
- Shaker
- 3/4 ounce gin
- 3/4 ounce Canadian whiskey
- 3/4 ounce lemon juice
- 1 dash Angostura bitters

AROMATIC DRINK

Shake the ingredients together, with ice, in the shaker and strain into the glass.

QUEEN'S COCKTAIL

- Cocktail glass
- Shaker
- 3/4 ounce gin
- 3/4 ounce pineapple juice
- 2 tsp. sweet red vermouth
- 2 tsp. dry vermouth

FRUITY APERITIF

Shake the ingredients together, with ice, in the shaker and strain into the cocktail glass.

XANTHIA

- Cocktail glass
- Mixing glass
- 3/4 ounce gin
- 3/4 ounce green Chartreuse
- 3/4 ounce cherry brandy

SWEET APERITIF

Mix the ingredients together, with ice, in the mixing glass and strain into the cocktail glass.

GIN

BRONX

- Cocktail glass
- Shaker
- 3/4 ounce gin
- 2 tsp. sweet red vermouth
- 2 tsp. dry vermouth
- 3/4 ounce orange juice

DRY, SHORT APERITIF

Shake all the ingredients together firmly, with ice cubes, in the shaker and strain into the cocktail glass.

ZAZA

- Cocktail glass
- Mixing glass
- I ounce gin
- I ounce Dubonnet
- I dash Angostura bitters

DRY APERITIF

Shake the ingredients together, with ice, in the shaker and strain into the cocktail glass.

NET ROLLER

- Champagne flute
- Shaker
- 3/4 ounce gin
- 3/4 ounce passion-fruit flavored liqueur
- 3/4 ounce orange juice
- Dry sparkling wine for topping up
GARNISH
- 1/2 slice of orange
- I maraschino cherry

REFRESHING, FRUITY CHAMPAGNE COCKTAIL FOR A RECEPTION

Shake all the ingredients, except the sparkling wine, together, with ice, in the shaker. Strain into the champagne flute and top up with sparkling wine. Perch the slice of orange on the rim of the glass. Fasten the cherry to the slice of orange with a toothpick.

Bronx

GIN

St. Vincent

Spicy, sweet after-dinner drink

- Cocktail glass
- Shaker
- 3/4 ounce gin
- 3/4 ounce light cream
- 3/4 ounce Galliano
- 3 dashes grenadine

Shake all the ingredients together well, with ice, in the mixing glass and strain into the glass.

Orange Flip

Creamy drink for the afternoon

- Goblet
- Shaker
- 1 1/2 ounces orange gin
- 3/4 ounce gin
- 3/4 ounce triple sec
- 2 tsp. light cream
- 1 egg yolk
- Extra: Grated nutmeg

Shake the ingredients together firmly, with ice, in the shaker and strain into the goblet. Sprinkle grated nutmeg on top.

Honolulu

Mild, fruity drink for the evening

- Cocktail glass
- Shaker
- 3/4 ounce gin
- 2 tsp. Benedictine
- 2 tsp. maraschino

Shake all the ingredients together, with ice, in the shaker and strain into the glass.

CLARIDGE

- Cocktail glass
- Mixing glass
- 1/2 ounce gin
- 1/2 ounce dry vermouth
- 2 tsp. apricot brandy
- 2 tsp. triple sec

GARNISH
- 1 maraschino cherry

MEDIUM-DRY DRINK FOR ANY OCCASION

Mix the ingredients together, with ice, in the mixing glass and strain into the glass. Add the cherry to the glass.

RHINE GOLD

- Cocktail glass
- Mixing glass
- 3/4 ounce gin
- 1/2 ounce Cointreau or other orange-flavored liqueur
- 2 tsp. dry vermouth
- 2 tsp. Campari

GARNISH
- 1 piece of orange peel

DRY, SLIGHTLY BITTER APERITIF

Mix the ingredients together, with ice, in the mixing glass and strain into the cocktail glass. Squeeze the orange peel over the drink.

BIJOU

- Cocktail glass
- Mixing glass
- 1 ounce gin
- 3/4 ounce dry vermouth
- 2 tsp. green Chartreuse

SPICY, AFTER-DINNER DRINK

Mix all the ingredients together, with ice cubes, in the mixing glass and strain into the cocktail glass.

GIN

DRY MARTINI

- Cocktail glass
- Mixing glass
- 1 1/2 ounces gin
- 3/4 ounce dry vermouth

GARNISH
- 1 slice of lemon
- 1 olive

DRY APERITIF

Mix the ingredients together, with ice, in the mixing glass and strain into the cocktail glass. Spear the olive on a toothpick and add it to the glass, with the lemon slice as garnish.

EXTRA-DRY MARTINI

- Cocktail glass
- Mixing glass
- 1 3/4 ounces gin
- 2 tsp. dry vermouth

GARNISH
- 1 olive
- 1 piece of lemon peel

VERY STRONG APERITIF

Mix the ingredients together, with ice, in the mixing glass and strain into the cocktail glass. Spear the olive on a toothpick add it to the glass, and squeeze the lemon peel over the drink.

SWEET MARTINI

- Cocktail glass
- Mixing glass
- 1 1/2 ounces gin
- 3/4 ounce sweet red vermouth

GARNISH
- 1 maraschino cherry
- 1 piece of lemon peel

SWEET APERITIF

Mix the ingredients together, with ice, in the mixing glass and strain into the cocktail glass. Spear the cherry on a toothpick and add it to the glass, and, if liked, squeeze the lemon peel over the drink.

Dry Martini

GIN

MANDY

MEDIUM-DRY APERITIF

- Cocktail shaker
- Shaker
- 1 ounce plus 1 tsp. orange juice
- 3/4 ounce gin
- 1 tsp. peach-flavored liqueur
- 1 tsp. orange curaçao
- 1 tsp. lemon juice

GARNISH
- 1 maraschino cherry
- 1 sprig of mint

Shake the ingredients together, with ice, in the shaker and strain into the cocktail glass. Perch the cherry and sprig of mint on the rim of the glass.

ANGEL'S FACE

SWEET APERITIF

- Cocktail glass
- Mixing glass
- 3/4 ounce gin
- 3/4 ounce Calvados
- 3/4 ounce apricot brandy

Shake the ingredients together, with ice, in the mixing glass and strain into the cocktail glass.

BALLA BALLA

DRY, BITTER CHAMPAGNE COCKTAIL FOR A RECEPTION

- Champagne flute
- Mixing glass
- 1/2 ounce gin
- 1/2 ounce triple sec
- 1/2 ounce Campari
- Dry champagne or sparkling wine for topping up

GARNISH
- 1/2 slice of orange
- 1 maraschino cherry

Mix all the ingredients, except the champagne, together, with ice, in the mixing glass. Strain into the champagne glass and top up with champagne. Add the fruit to the glass.

GIMLET

- Cocktail glass
- Mixing glass
- 1 1/2 ounces gin
- 3/4 ounce lime juice cordial
- Extra: 1 maraschino cherry, 1 piece of lime peel, and 1 piece of lemon peel

SLIGHTLY DRY APERITIF

Mix the ingredients together, with plenty of ice, in the mixing glass and strain into the cocktail glass. Add the cherry to the glass. Squeeze the lime and lemon peels over the drink and add the peel to the glass.

PARADISE

- Cocktail glass
- Shaker
- 3/4 ounce gin
- 3/4 ounce apricot brandy
- 3/4 ounce orange juice

MEDIUM-DRY, FRUITY AFTER-DINNER DRINK

Shake the ingredients together, with ice, in the shaker and strain into the cocktail glass.

EXTERMINATOR

- Large champagne flute
- Shaker
- 1 1/2 ounces grapefruit juice
- 1 ounce gin
- 3/4 ounce Cointreau or other orange-flavored liqueur
- Dry champagne or sparkling wine for topping up

GARNISH
- 1 maraschino cherry

DRY CHAMPAGNE COCKTAIL FOR A RECEPTION

Shake the ingredients, except the champagne, together, with ice, in the shaker. Strain into the champagne glass and top up with sparkling wine. Add the cherry to the glass.

GIN

CARIBBEAN SUNSET

SWEET AFTER-DINNER DRINK

- Goblet
- Shaker
- 1/2 ounce gin
- 1/2 ounce crème de banane
- 1/2 ounce blue curaçao
- 1/2 ounce fresh cream
- 1/2 ounce lemon juice
- 1 dash grenadine

Shake the ingredients together, with ice, in the shaker. Strain into a large goblet.

HAPPY BIRTHDAY

FRUITY, CHAMPAGNE COCKTAIL FOR A RECEPTION

- Champagne flute
- Shaker
- 1 1/2 ounces gin
- 1/2 ounce orange curaçao
- 1/2 ounce light rum
- 1/2 ounce peach-flavored liqueur
- 1/2 ounce pineapple juice
- Champagne or sparkling wine for topping up
GARNISH
- 1/2 slice of lemon
- 1 maraschino cherry

Shake all the ingredients, except the champagne, together, with ice, in the shaker and strain into the champagne flute. Top up with the champagne. Perch the slice of lemon on the rim of the glass and fasten the cherry to it with a toothpick.

TOM COLLINS

FRUITY, TANGY DRINK FOR HOT DAYS

- Collins/highball glass
- 1 1/2 ounces gin
- 3/4 ounce lemon juice
- 2 tsp. sugar syrup
- Soda water for topping up
GARNISH
- 1/2 slice of lemon
- 1 maraschino cherry

Mix all the ingredients together, except the soda water, with ice, in the Collins glass and top up with the soda water. Perch the slice of lemon on the rim of the glass, add a cherry to the glass. Serve with a long stirrer.

Caribbean Sunset

GIN

GIN AND FRENCH

- Cocktail glass
- Mixing glass
- 1 1/2 ounces gin
- 3/4 ounce dry French vermouth
- Extra: 1 piece of lemon peel

VERY DRY APERITIF

Mix the ingredients together, with ice, in the mixing glass and strain into the cocktail glass. Squeeze the lemon peel over the drink and add the peel to the glass.

MAXIM

- Cocktail glass
- Mixing glass
- 1 ounce gin
- 3/4 ounce sweet red vermouth
- 2 tsp. white crème de cacao

SPICY, MILD AFTER-DINNER DRINK

Mix the ingredients together, with ice, in the mixing glass and strain into the glass.

INES

- Cocktail glass
- Mixing glass
- 3/4 ounce gin
- 3/4 ounce dry vermouth
- 3/4 ounce sweet red vermouth
- 2 tsp. amaretto
GARNISH
- 1 green olive, stuffed with pimiento

MEDIUM-DRY APERITIF

Mix the ingredients together, with ice, in the mixing glass and strain into the cocktail glass. Add the olive to the glass.

TANGO

MEDIUM-DRY APERITIF

- Champagne or cocktail glass
- Shaker
- 1 ounce gin
- 1/2 ounce sweet red vermouth
- 1/2 ounce dry vermouth
- 2 tsp. orange juice
- 2 dashes orange curaçao
- Extra: 1 piece of orange peel

Shake the ingredients together, with ice, in the shaker and strain into the glass. Add the piece of orange peel to the glass.

GIN AND IT

MEDIUM-DRY APERITIF

- Cocktail glass
- Mixing glass
- 1 ounce gin
- 1 ounce sweet red vermouth

GARNISH
- 1 maraschino cherry

Mix the ingredients together, with plenty of ice, in the mixing glass and strain into the cocktail glass. Spear the cherry on a toothpick and add it to the glass.

BLUE DEVIL

FRUITY, MILD DRINK FOR A PARTY

- Cocktail glass
- Shaker
- 1 1/2 ounces gin
- 3/4 ounce blue curaçao
- 3/4 ounce lemon juice
- 2 tsp. sugar syrup

GARNISH
- 1 maraschino cherry

Mix the ingredients together, with ice cubes, in the shaker and strain into the cocktail glass. Perch the cherry on the rim of the glass.

WATERMELON SLING

SWEET, REFRESHING DRINK

- Cocktail glass
- Blender
- 1/4 watermelon
- 1 ounce gin
- 1 tsp. sugar
- Juice of 1/2 a lime

Discard the seeds from a watermelon. Scoop the flesh into a blender and add the ingredients. Blend until smooth and pour into the glass.

ALEXANDRA

SWEET DRINK FOR THE AFTERNOON

- Champagne or cocktail glass
- Shaker
- 3/4 ounce gin
- 3/4 ounce white or brown crème de cacao
- 3/4 ounce light cream

Shake all the ingredients together, with ice, in the shaker and strain into the glass.

PALL MALL

SPICY APERITIF

- Cocktail glass
- Mixing glass
- 1 1/2 ounces gin
- 2 tsp. sweet red vermouth
- 2 tsp. dry vermouth
GARNISH
- 1 maraschino cherry

Mix the ingredients together, with ice, in the mixing glass and strain into the cocktail glass. Add the cherry to the glass.

Watermelon Sling

GIN

FRENCH 75

AROMATIC APERITIF OR AFTER-DINNER DRINK

- Champagne flute
- Shaker
- 3/4 ounce gin
- 3/4 ounce Cointreau
- 3/4 ounce lemon juice
- 1 dash Pernod
- Champagne or sparkling wine for topping up

GARNISH
- 1/2 slice of orange
- 1 maraschino cherry

Shake all the ingredients, except the champagne, together, with ice, in the shaker and strain into the champagne glass. Top up with the champagne. Spear the slice of orange and cherry on a toothpick, and perch the garnish on the rim of the glass.

ISLE OF SKYE

SWEET APERITIF

- Cocktail glass
- Shaker
- 3/4 ounces gin
- 3/4 ounce Drambuie
- 3/4 ounce lemon juice

Shake the ingredients together, with ice, in the shaker and strain into the cocktail glass.

TROPICAL SUN

LIGHT, FRUITY, REFRESHING DRINK FOR A SUMMER PARTY

- Highball/Collins glass
- Shaker
- 1 1/2 ounces gin
- 3/4 ounce passion-fruit syrup
- 2 tsp. lemon juice
- Tropical bitters
- 1 dash grenadine

GARNISH
- 1/2 slice of orange
- 1 maraschino cherry

Shake all the ingredients together, except the tropical bitters and grenadine, together, with ice, in the shaker and strain into the highball glass over ice cubes. Top up with tropical bitters. Float the grenadine on top of the drink. Spear the slice of orange and the cherry on a long wooden skewer and add it to the drink.

ALASKA

- Cocktail glass
- Mixing glass
- 1 1/2 ounces gin
- 3/4 ounce yellow Chartreuse
- Extra: 1 piece of lemon peel

AROMATIC APERITIF

Mix the ingredients together, with ice, in the mixing glass, strain into the cocktail glass and squeeze the lemon peel over the drink.

ADAM AND EVE

- Champagne or cocktail glass
- Shaker
- 3/4 ounce gin
- 3/4 ounce Drambuie
- 3/4 ounce Angostura bitters
- 2 tsp. lemon juice
- 1 dash grenadine

GARNISH
- 1 slice of lemon
- 1 maraschino cherry

FRUITY, SPICY DRINK FOR THE EVENING

Shake all the ingredients together, with ice cubes, in the shaker and strain into the glass. Spear the fruit on a toothpick and lay the garnish across the rim of the glass.

MAR DEL PLATA

- Cocktail glass
- Mixing glass
- 1 ounce gin
- 3/4 ounce dry vermouth
- 2 tsp. Benedictine
- Extra: 1 piece of lemon peel

MEDIUM-DRY APERITIF

Mix the ingredients together, with ice, in the mixing glass and strain into the glass. Squeeze the lemon peel over the drink.

GIN

RED KISS

- Cocktail glass
- Shaker
- 1/2 ounce gin
- 1/2 ounce cherry brandy
- 1 ounce dry vermouth

GARNISH
- 1 lemon peel spiral
- 1 maraschino cherry

SWEET, DRY DRINK

Shake all the ingredients together, with ice, in the shaker and strain into the glass. Garnish with the fruit.

BANJINO

- Cocktail glass
- Shaker
- 1 ounce gin
- 1 ounce orange juice
- 1 dash banana-flavored liqueur

GARNISH
- 1 slice of orange

FRUITY, SPICY DRINK FOR A PARTY

Shake all the ingredients together, with ice, in the shaker and strain into the glass. Perch the slice of orange on the rim of the glass.

ROYAL

- Cocktail glass
- Shaker
- 3/4 ounce gin
- 3/4 ounce dry vermouth
- 3/4 ounce cherry brandy
- 1 dash maraschino

GARNISH
- 1 green maraschino cherry

FRUITY, SPICY APERITIF AND AFTER-DINNER DRINK

Shake all the ingredients together, with ice, in the shaker and strain into the cocktail glass. Perch the cherry on the rim of the glass.

Red Kiss

GIN

DRY GIBSON

DRY APERITIF

- Cocktail glass
- Mixing glass
- 1 1/2 ounces gin
- 3/4 ounce dry vermouth
GARNISH
- 2 pearl onions

Mix the ingredients together, with plenty of ice, in the mixing glass and strain into the cocktail glass. Spear the onions on a toothpick and add it to the glass.

ASTORIA

DRY, SPICY APERITIF

- Cocktail glass
- Mixing glass
- 1 1/2 ounces gin
- 3/4 ounce dry vermouth
- 2 dashes orange bitters
GARNISH
- 1 green olive

Mix all the ingredients together, with ice, in the mixing glass and strain into the glass. Add the olive to the glass.

PICCADILLY

SPICY, DELICATE DRY DRINK FOR THE EVENING OR AS AN APERITIF

- Cocktail glass
- Mixing glass
- 1 1/2 ounces gin
- 3/4 ounce dry vermouth
- 1 dash grenadine
- 1 dash Pernod

Mix all the ingredients together, with ice, in the mixing glass and strain into the glass.

MISSISSIPPI

- Cocktail glass
- Shaker
- 1 ounce gin
- 1 ounce crème de cassis
- 4 dashes orange juice

MILD, FRUITY DRINK FOR THE EVENING

Shake all the ingredients together, with ice, in the shaker and strain into the cocktail glass.

EMPIRE STATE

- Cocktail glass
- Mixing glass
- 1 1/2 ounces gin
- 3/4 ounce cognac
- 3/4 ounce apricot brandy
- 1 dash orange bitters

GARNISH
- 1 maraschino cherry

SPICY, DELICATE, DRY DRINK FOR THE EVENING

Mix the ingredients together, with ice, in the mixing glass and strain into the cocktail glass. Perch the cherry on the rim of the glass.

BERMUDA

- Cocktail glass
- Shaker
- 2 ounces gin
- 3/4 ounce peach brandy
- 1 tsp. blue curaçao

GARNISH
- 1/2 slice of orange

DELICATELY SPICY DRINK FOR ANY TIME OF THE YEAR

Shake all the ingredients together, with ice, in the shaker and strain into the cocktail glass. Perch the slice of orange on the rim of the glass.

GIN

SLOE GIN FIZZ

- Highball/Collins glass
- 1 1/2 ounces sloe gin
- Juice of 1 lemon
- 1 tsp. caster sugar
- Soda water

GARNISH
- 1 lemon peel spiral

BITTERSWEET, REFRESHING DRINK

Pour the ingredients, except the soda water, into the glass and stir to dissolve the caster sugar. Top up with soda water and garnish.

MOULIN ROUGE

- Cocktail glass
- Shaker
- 3/4 ounce gin
- 3/4 ounce apricot brandy
- 3/4 ounce lemon juice
- 1 tsp. grenadine

GARNISH
- 1 maraschino cherry

FRUITY, DELICATE DRY DRINK FOR ANY TIME OF THE YEAR

Shake all the ingredients together, with ice, in the shaker and strain into the cocktail glass. Add the cherry to the glass.

AFTER THE STORM

- Cocktail glass
- Shaker
- 3/4 ounce gin
- 3/4 ounce light cream
- 2 tsp. scotch
- 2 tsp. white crème de cacao

GARNISH
- 1 maraschino cherry

MILD, SPICY AFTER-DINNER DRINK

Shake all the ingredients together firmly, with ice, in the shaker and strain into the glass. Perch the cherry on the rim of the glass.

Sloe Gin Fizz

GIN

ENGLISH ROSE

MEDIUM-DRY APERITIF

- Cocktail glass
- Shaker
- 3/4 ounce gin
- 2 tsp. apricot brandy
- 2 tsp. dry vermouth
- 1 tsp. grenadine
- 3 dashes lemon juice

Shake the ingredients together, with ice, in the shaker and strain into the cocktail glass.

HABERFIELD

SPICY, DRY APERITIF

- Cocktail glass
- Shaker
- 1 1/2 ounces gin
- 2 tsp. dry vermouth
- 2 tsp. lemon juice

Shake all the ingredients together firmly, with ice cubes, in the shaker and strain into the cocktail glass.

BARNUM

MEDIUM-DRY APERITIF

- Cocktail glass
- Shaker
- 1 ounce gin
- 3/4 ounce apricot brandy
- 3 dashes lemon juice
- 2 dashes Angostura bitters

Shake the ingredients together, with ice, in the shaker and strain into the cocktail glass.

EXOTIC EXOTIC

- Rocks glass
- 1 ounce gin
- 1/2 ounce brown crème de cacao
- 1/2 ounce crème de banane

SWEET DRINK FOR THE EVENING

Mix the ingredients together, with ice cubes, in the glass and serve the drink with a stirrer.

GIN CRUSTA

- Paris goblet with sugared rim
- Mixing glass
- 1 1/2 ounces gin
- 2 tsp. cherry-flavored liqueur
- 2 dashes Angostura bitters

SPICY, FRUITY DRINK FOR ANY TIME OF YEAR

Mix the ingredients together, with ice cubes, in the mixing glass and strain into the sugar-rimmed glass.

JOHN COLLINS

- Collins/highball glass
- 1 1/2 ounces gin
- 3/4 ounce lemon juice
- 2 tsp. sugar syrup
- Soda water for topping up

GARNISH
- 1/2 slice of lemon
- 1 maraschino cherry

REFRESHING DRINK FOR HOT DAYS

Mix all the ingredients together, except the soda water, together, with ice cubes, in the glass and top up with the soda water. Perch the slice of lemon on the rim of the glass and add the cherry to the glass. Serve with a stirrer.

GIN

THE VISITOR

- Cocktail glass
- Shaker
- 1/2 ounce gin
- 1/2 ounce Cointreau
- 1/2 ounce crème de banane
- I dash of fresh orange juice
- I egg white

GARNISH
- Banana slices
- Twisted orange slices

REFRESHING, FRUITY DRINK

Shake all the ingredients together, with ice, in the shaker and strain into the glass. Decorate with the fruit.

SINGAPORE SLING

- Highball/Collins glass
- Shaker
- I ounce gin
- 2 tsp. cherry heering
- I dash Bendictine
- I dash Cointreau
- I dash Angostura bitters
- Lime and pineapple juice for topping up

GARNISH
- I piece of pineapple
- I maraschino cherry

FRUITY DRINK FOR HOT DAYS

Shake all the ingredients, except the fruit juices, with ice, in the shaker and strain into the glass over ice. Top up with lime and pineapple juices. Spear the pineapple and cherry on a toothpick. Lay the garnish across the rim of the glass.

SINGAPORE GIN SLING

- Highball/Collins glass
- Shaker
- I 1/2 ounces gin
- 3/4 ounce cherry heering
- 3/4 ounce lemon juice
- Soda water for topping up

GARNISH
- 1/2 slice of lemon
- I maraschino cherry

REFRESHING DRINK FOR HOT DAYS

Shake all the ingredients, except the soda water, with ice, in the shaker and strain into the glass over ice. Top up with soda water. Spear the lemon slice and cherry on a toothpick. Lay the garnish across the rim of the glass.

The Visitor

GIN

NEPTUNE'S FAIR

FRUITY, REFRESHING DRINK FOR A PARTY

- Highball/Collins glass
- Shaker
- 3/4 ounce gin
- 3/4 ounce lemon juice
- 2 tsp. Pisang Ambon
- 2 tsp. passion-fruit liqueur
- Bitter lemon for topping up

GARNISH
- 1 slice of lemon
- 1 green maraschino cherry
- 1 small sprig of mint

Shake all the ingredients, except the bitter lemon, together, with ice, in the shaker and strain into the highball glass over ice. Top up with the bitter lemon. Perch the slice of lemon on the rim of the glass and fasten the cherry to it with a toothpick. Add the sprig of mint to the glass.

GIN BUCK

FRUITY, SPICY DRINK FOR ANY TIME OF THE YEAR

- Rocks glass
- 1 1/2 ounces gin
- 3/4 ounce lemon juice
- Ginger ale for topping up

Mix the gin and lemon juice together in the glass, top up with ginger ale, and stir briefly.

SOUTH PACIFIC

FRUITY, REFRESHING DRINK FOR A SUMMER PARTY

- Highball/Collins glass
- 3/4 ounce gin
- 2 tsp. blue curaçao
- 2 tsp. Galliano
- Bitter lemon for topping up

GARNISH
- 1 maraschino cherry
- 1 sprig of mint

Mix all the ingredients, except the bitter lemon, together, with ice cubes, in the highball glass. Top up with bitter lemon. Add the cherry and the sprig of mint to the glass and serve the drink with a stirrer.

AMBER GLOW

- Rocks glass
- 1 ounce gin
- 1 ounce light rum
- 1 ounce lime juice
- 1 tsp. grenadine
- Soda water for topping up

FRUITY, DRY DRINK FOR A SUMMER PARTY

Mix together the ingredients, except the soda water, in the glass. Top up with soda water and stir briefly.

GIN SOUR

- Rocks glass
- Shaker
- 1 1/2 ounces gin
- 3/4 ounce lemon juice
- 2 tsp. sugar syrup
- Soda water for topping up

GARNISH
- 1/2 slice of lemon
- 1 maraschino cherry

STRONG, REFRESHING SOUR FOR A PARTY

Shake all the ingredients, except the soda water, together, with ice, in the shaker and strain into the glass. Add the slice of lemon and the cherry to the glass. Top up with soda water.

PARK LANE

- Rocks glass
- Shaker
- 1 1/2 ounces gin
- 1 1/2 ounces orange juice
- 3/4 ounce apricot brandy
- 1 dash grenadine
- 1 dash lemon juice

FRUITY, MILD DRINK FOR A PARTY

Shake all the ingredients together, with ice cubes, in the shaker and strain into the glass.

GIN

SNAKE IN THE GRASS

- Cocktail glass
- Shaker
- 1/2 ounce gin
- 1/2 ounce Cointreau
- 1/2 ounce dry vermouth
- 1/2 ounce lemon juice

DRY, BITTER DRINK

Shake all the ingredients together, with ice cubes, in the shaker and strain into the glass.

AMOUR MARIE

- Cocktail glass
- Mixing glass
- 1 ounce gin
- 1/2 ounce Parfait Amour
- 1/2 ounce dry vermouth
GARNISH
- 1 maraschino cherry

FRUITY DRINK FOR THE SUMMER

Mix the ingredients together, with ice, in the mixing glass and strain into the cocktail glass. Add the cherry to the glass.

LEMON FLIP

- Champagne flute
- Shaker
- 1 1/2 ounces lemon juice
- 1 ounce gin
- 3/4 ounce triple sec
- 1 egg yolk
GARNISH
- 1/2 slice of lemon

REFRESHING, AFTER-DINNER DRINK

Shake the ingredients together firmly, with ice, in the shaker and strain into the champagne flute. Perch the slice of lemon on the rim of the glass.

Snake in the Grass

GIN

PINK ROSE

FRUITY DRINK FOR ANY TIME OF YEAR

- Cocktail glass
- Shaker
- 1 1/2 ounces gin
- 1 tsp. grenadine
- 1 tsp. lemon juice
- 1 tsp. light cream
- 1 egg white

Shake all the ingredients together, with ice, in the shaker and strain well into the cocktail glass.

GIN AND SIN

FRUITY, SPICY DRINK FOR ANY TIME OF THE YEAR

- Rocks glass
- Shaker
- 1 1/2 ounces gin
- 3/4 ounce orange juice
- 3/4 ounce lemon juice
- 2 tsp. grenadine
GARNISH
- 1/2 slice of orange

Shake all the ingredients together firmly, with ice, in the shaker and strain into the glass. Perch the slice of orange on the rim of the glass.

BROWN LADY

FRUITY, DRY DRINK FOR ANY TIME OF THE YEAR

- Champagne or cocktail glass
- Shaker
- 1 ounce gin
- 1/2 ounce Grand Marnier
- 1/2 ounce lemon juice
GARNISH
- 1/2 slice of orange

Shake all the ingredients together, with ice cubes, in the shaker and strain into the glass. Add the slice of orange to the glass.

BERMUDA ROSE

DRY APERITIF

- Cocktail glass
- Shaker
- 1 1/2 ounces gin
- 2 tsp. lemon juice
- 1 tsp. apricot brandy
- 2 dashes grenadine

Shake the ingredients together, with ice, in the shaker and strain into the glass.

VIRGIN

SWEET AFTER-DINNER DRINK

- Cocktail glass
- Mixing glass
- 3/4 ounce gin
- 3/4 ounce white crème de menthe
- 3/4 ounce triple sec

Mix the ingredients together, with ice, in the mixing glass and strain into the cocktail glass.

CONCORDE

FRUITY, DELICATE DRY DRINK FOR ANY TIME OF THE YEAR

- Cocktail glass
- Shaker
- 1 ounce gin
- 2 tsp. apricot brandy
- 2 tsp. Campari
- 2 tsp. grenadine

GARNISH
- 1 maraschino cherry

Shake all the ingredients together, with ice cubes, in the shaker and strain into the cocktail glass. Perch the cherry on the rim of the glass.

STRAWBERRY DAWN

FRUITY, SWEET DRINK

- Cocktail glass
- Blender
- 1 ounce gin
- 1 ounce coconut cream
- 3 large strawberries
- Lime or lemon juice to taste

GARNISH
- 1 strawberry

Mix the ingredients together, except the lemon or lime juice, in a blender. Add lime or lemon juice to taste. Pour into a cocktail glass. Garnish the glass with the fruit. Serve with straws.

WESTERN ROSE

TANGY, DRY DRINK FOR THE EVENING

- Cocktail glass
- Shaker
- 3/4 ounce gin
- 2 tsp. apricot brandy
- 2 tsp. dry vermouth
- 3 dashes lemon juice

Shake the ingredients together, with ice, in the shaker and strain into the cocktail glass.

DERBY

APERITIF

- Cocktail glass
- Mixing glass
- 2 ounces gin
- 2 dashes peach bitters

GARNISH
- A few mint leaves

Mix all the ingredients together, with ice cubes, in the mixing glass and strain into the cocktail glass. Add the mint leaves to the glass.

Strawberry Dawn

GIN

LADY CHATTERLEY

MEDIUM-DRY APERITIF

- Champagne glass
- Shaker
- 1 ounce gin
- 2 tsp. triple sec
- 2 tsp. dry vermouth
- 2 tsp. orange juice

Shake the ingredients together, with ice, in the shaker and strain into the glass.

SPENCER

MEDIUM-DRY APERITIF

- Cocktail glass
- Shaker
- 3/4 ounce gin
- 3/4 ounce apricot brandy
- 1 tsp. orange juice
- 1 dash Angostura bitters

Shake the ingredients together, with ice, in the shaker and strain into the glass.

JOURNALIST

MEDIUM-DRY DRINK FOR ALL OCCASIONS

- Cocktail glass
- Shaker
- 1 ounce gin
- 2 tsp. dry vermouth
- 2 tsp. sweet red vermouth
- 1 tsp. triple sec
- 1 tsp. lemon juice
- 1 dash Angostura bitters

Shake the ingredients together, with ice, in the shaker and strain into the glass.

HORSE'S NECK

DELICATE, DRY DRINK FOR ANY TIME OF THE YEAR

- Large rocks glass
- 1 1/2 ounces gin
- 2 tsp. grenadine
- Ginger ale for topping up

GARNISH

- 1 lemon peel spiral

Mix the gin and grenadine together, with ice cubes, in the glass. Top up with ginger ale and stir briefly. Hang the lemon peel spiral over the rim of the glass.

PIMM'S ROYAL

REFRESHING DRINK FOR THE SUMMER

- Highball/Collins glass
- 1 1/2 ounces Pimm's No. 1
- Champagne or sparkling wine for topping up
- 1 piece of cucumber peel
- 2 maraschino cherries
- 1/2 slice of orange
- 1/2 slice of lemon

Pour the Pimm's No. 1 into the highball glass over ice cubes. Top up with champagne or sparkling wine. Add the cucumber peel and fruit to the glass.

CHAMPAGNE FIZZ

SPARKLING LIGHT FIZZY DRINK FOR A PARTY

- Champagne flute
- Shaker
- 1 ounce gin
- 3/4 ounce lemon juice
- 2 tsp. sugar syrup
- 2 ounces champagne or sparkling wine

GARNISH

- 1/2 slice of lemon

Shake all the ingredients, except the champagne, together, with ice, in the shaker. Strain into the flute and top up with champagne. Perch the slice of lemon on the rim of the glass.

GIN

RED BARON

- Cocktail glass
- Shaker
- 2 ounce gin
- 1/2 ounce orange juice
- 1 dash grenadine
- 1 dash lemon juice
- 1 dash lime juice
- 1 dash sugar syrup

GARNISH
- 1 orange peel spiral

BITTERSWEET TASTY DRINK

Shake all the ingredients together, with ice, in the shaker and strain into the cocktail glass.

OPTIMIST

- Highball/Collins glass
- Shaker
- 1 ounce gin
- 3/4 ounce crème de cassis
- 3/4 ounce pineapple juice
- Orange juice for topping up
- 1 dash passion-fruit syrup

GARNISH
- 1/2 slice of orange
- 1 piece of pineapple
- 1 green maraschino cherry

FRUITY DRINK FOR ANY OCCASION

Shake all the ingredients, except the passion-fruit syrup and orange juice, together, with ice, in the shaker and strain into the highball glass over ice cubes. Top up with orange juice. Float the passion-fruit syrup on top of the drink. Spear the fruit on a toothpick and lay the garnish across the rim of the glass.

GOLD DIGGER

- Highball/Collins glass
- Mixing glass
- 1/2 ounce gin
- 1/2 ounce kiwi-fruit-flavored liqueur
- 1/2 ounce melon-flavored liqueur
- 1/2 ounce Aperol
- Orange juice for topping up

FRUITY DRINK FOR A PARTY

Mix all the ingredients, except the orange juice, together, with ice, in the mixing glass and pour into the highball glass over ice. Top up with orange juice and stir well. Serve with a stirrer.

Red Baron

GIN

NEW ORLEANS FIZZ

FRUITY, REFRESHING FIZZ FOR A SUMMER PARTY

- Highball/Collins glass
- Shaker
- 1 1/2 ounces gin
- 3/4 ounce lemon juice
- 2 tsp. sugar syrup
- 2 tsp. light cream
- 3 dashes orange bitters
- 1 egg white
- Soda water for topping up

Shake all the ingredients, except the soda water, together firmly, with ice, in the shaker and strain into the highball glass. Top up with soda water.

SILVER FIZZ

REFRESHING, FRUITY FIZZ FOR THE SUMMER

- Highball/Collins glass
- Shaker
- 1 1/2 ounces gin
- 3/4 ounce lemon juice
- 2 tsp. sugar syrup
- 1 egg white
- Soda water for topping up

Shake all the ingredients, except the soda water, together, with ice, in the shaker and strain into the highball glass. Top up with soda water.

SEVEN SEAS

FRUITY DRINK FOR A SUMMER PARTY

- Highball/Collins glass
- 1 1/2 ounces Pisang Ambon
- 3/4 ounce gin
- 1 dash crème de banane
- Tonic water for topping up
GARNISH
- 1 maraschino cherry

Mix the ingredients together, with ice cubes, in the highball glass. Add the cherry to the glass and serve the drink with a stirrer.

JOHNNIE RED

FRUITY DRINK FOR THE SUMMER

- Highball/Collins glass
- 1 ounce gin
- 1/2 ounce Parfait Amour
- 1/2 ounce crème de banane
- 1 dash grenadine
- Orange juice for topping up

GARNISH
- 1 orange peel spiral

Mix the ingredients together, with ice cubes, in the highball glass. Hang the orange peel spiral over the rim of the glass and serve the drink with a long stirrer.

LADY KILLER

FRUITY, SWEET DRINK FOR THE SUMMER

- Highball/Collins glass
- Shaker
- 1 ounce passion-fruit juice
- 1 ounce pineapple juice
- 3/4 ounce gin
- 2 tsp. Cointreau
- 2 tsp. apricot brandy

GARNISH
- 1 green plum
- 1 orange peel spiral
- 1 sprig of mint

Shake all the ingredients together firmly, with ice, in the shaker and strain into the highball glass over ice cubes. Perch the plum on the rim of the glass. Spear the orange peel spiral on a toothpick and lay the garnish across the rim of the glass. Add the sprig of mint to the glass.

BLUE EYES

SPICY, MILD DRINK FOR A PARTY

- Highball/Collins glass
- 1 ounce gin
- 3/4 ounce sweet white vermouth
- 2 tsp. blue curaçao
- Ginger ale for topping up

GARNISH
- 1 slice of orange
- 1 maraschino cherry

Mix the gin, vermouth, and curaçao together, with ice cubes, in the highball glass. Top up with ginger ale and stir again. Perch the orange slice on the rim of the glass and fasten the cherry to the slice of orange with a toothpick.

GIN

ROSE

- Cocktail glass
- Shaker
- 1 1/2 ounces gin
- 1/2 ounce cherry brandy
- 1/2 ounce dry vermouth

GARNISH
- 1 maraschino cherry

FRUITY, DRY DRINK

Shake all the ingredients together, with ice, in the shaker and strain into the glass. Add the cherry as a garnish.

BULLDOG COOLER

- Highball/Collins glass
- Shaker
- 1 ounce gin
- 1 ounce orange juice
- 2 tsp. triple sec
- Ginger ale for topping up

GARNISH
- 1 slice of orange

FRUITY, MILD DRINK FOR HOT DAYS

Shake the gin, orange juice, and curaçao together, with ice cubes, in the shaker and strain into the highball glass. Top up with the ginger ale and stir briefly. Perch the slice of orange on the rim of the glass.

STROUMF

- Highball/Collins glass
- Shaker
- 3/4 ounce gin
- 3/4 ounce apricot brandy
- 2 tsp. amaretto
- 1 dash lemon juice
- Orange juice for topping up

FULL-FLAVORED DRINK FOR THE EVENING

Shake all the ingredients, except the orange juice, together, with ice, in the shaker and strain into the highball glass. Top up with the orange juice and stir. Serve with a stirrer.

Rose

GIN

GOLDEN FIZZ

REFRESHING FIZZ FOR THE SUMMER

- Highball/Collins glass
- Shaker
- 1 1/2 ounces gin
- 3/4 ounce lemon juice
- 2 tsp. sugar syrup
- 1 egg yolk
- Soda water for topping up

Shake all the ingredients, except the soda water, together, with plenty of ice, in the shaker and pour into the highball glass. Top up with the soda water.

MESSICANO

FRUITY, SWEET DRINK FOR A SUMMER PARTY

- Highball/Collins glass
- Shaker
- 3/4 ounce gin
- 3/4 ounce Galliano
- 3/4 ounce orange juice
- 1 tsp. amaretto
GARNISH
- 1 slice of orange
- 1 maraschino cherry
- 1 sprig of mint

Shake all the ingredients together, with ice, in the shaker and strain into the highball glass over ice cubes. Perch the fruit and sprig of mint on the rim of the glass.

LONDON FEVER

MILD, FRUITY DRINK FOR A PARTY

- Rocks glass
- 1 ounce gin
- 1 ounce lime cordial
- 3/4 ounce light rum
- 1 tsp. grenadine
- Soda water for topping up
GARNISH
- 1/2 slice of pineapple
- 1 maraschino cherry

Mix all the ingredients, except the soda water, together, with ice, in the glass. Top up with the soda water and stir briefly. Perch the fruit on the rim of the glass.

MINT FIZZ

SPICY, FRESH DRINK FOR ANY TIME OF YEAR

- Highball/Collins glass
- Shaker
- 1 3/4 ounces gin
- 1 ounce lemon juice
- 3/4 ounce sugar syrup
- 2 tsp. green crème de menthe
- Soda water for topping up

Shake all the ingredients together, except the soda water, long and firmly, with ice cubes, in the shaker. Strain into the highball glass and add a few ice cubes. Top up with the soda water and stir briefly.

APRICOT BLOSSOM

BITTER, REFRESHING DRINK FOR THE EVENING

- Highball/Collins glass
- Shaker
- 3/4 ounce gin
- 3/4 ounce apricot-flavored liqueur
- 1 tsp. lime juice
- 2 dashes Angostura bitters
- Tonic water for topping up

GARNISH
- 1 slice of lime

Shake all the ingredients, except the tonic water, together, with ice, in the shaker and strain into the highball glass and stir. Perch the slice of lime on the rim of the glass. Serve the drink immediately.

POGO STICK

TANGY, REFRESHING DRINK FOR THE SUMMER

- Highball/Collins glass
- Shaker
- 1 ounce gin
- 2 ounces grapefruit juice
- 3/4 ounce Cointreau
- 2 tsp. lemon juice

GARNISH
- 1/2 grapefruit segment

Shake all the ingredients together, with ice, in the shaker and strain into the highball glass over ice cubes. Perch the grapefruit segment on the rim of the glass.

GIN

ETON BLAZER

- Rocks glass
- Shaker
- 1 1/4 ounces gin
- 1/3 ounce kirsch
- 2 tbsp. lemon juice
- 1–2 tbsp. powdered sugar
- Soda water for topping up

GARNISH
- 1 twist of lemon

REFRESHING DRINK FOR A HOT DAY

Shake all the ingredients, except the soda water, together with ice, in the shaker and strain into the glass. Top up with soda water.

PARADISO

- Highball/Collins glass
- Shaker
- 1 ounce gin
- 3/4 ounce apricot brandy
- 2 tsp. orange juice

GARNISH
- 1 slice of orange

FRUITY, SPICY DRINK FOR A SUMMER PARTY

Shake all the ingredients together firmly, with ice, in the shaker and strain into the highball glass over ice cubes. Perch the slice of orange on the rim of the glass.

STARMANIA

- Highball/Collins glass
- Shaker
- 3/4 ounce gin
- 2 tsp. apricot brandy
- 2 tsp. passion-fruit juice
- 1 tsp. Campari
- 1 dash green curaçao
- Ginger ale for topping up

GARNISH
- Small pieces of fruit

SWEET DRINK FOR A PARTY

Shake all the ingredients, except the ginger ale, together, with ice, in the shaker and strain into the highball glass over ice. Top up with ginger ale and stir. Spear the pieces of fruit on a toothpick and lay the garnish across the rim of the glass. Serve with an attractive stirrer.

Eton Blazer

GIN

SWEET MARY

REFRESHING DRINK FOR HOT DAYS

- Highball/Collins glass
- 1 3/4 ounces crème de banane
- 1/2 ounce gin
- 1 dash crème de cassis
- Lemonade for topping up

GARNISH
- 1 maraschino cherry

Mix all the ingredients, except the lemonade, together, with ice cubes, in the highball glass. Top up with lemonade. Spear the maraschino cherry on a toothpick and lay the garnish across the rim of the glass.

RED SUNSHINE

FRUITY, DELICATE, DRY DRINK FOR A PARTY

- Highball/Collins glass
- Shaker
- 1 ounce gin
- 3/4 ounce blackcurrant-flavored liqueur
- 3/4 ounce lemon juice
- Soda water for topping up

Shake the gin, blackcurrant liqueur, and lemon juice together, with ice, in the shaker and strain into the glass over ice cubes. Top up with soda water and stir briefly.

ROYAL FIZZ

REFRESHING FIZZ FOR HOT DAYS

- Highball/Collins glass
- Shaker
- 1 1/2 ounces gin
- 3/4 ounce lemon juice
- 2 tsp. sugar syrup
- 1 egg
- Soda water for topping up

Shake all the ingredients, except the soda water, together firmly, with ice, in the shaker and strain into the highball glass. Slowly top up with soda water.

ROSETTE MEROLA

- Highball/Collins glass
- 1/2 ounce gin
- 1/2 ounce Gold Digger liqueur
- 1/2 ounce kiwi-fruit-flavored liqueur
- 1/2 Aperol
- Orange juice for topping up

GARNISH
- 1 maraschino cherry
- 1 piece of orange peel

FRUITY DRINK FOR A PARTY

Mix all the ingredients together, except the orange juice, together, with ice cubes, in the highball glass. Top up with the orange juice. Spear the cherry and the orange peel on a toothpick and lay the garnish across the rim of the glass. Serve the drink with a stirrer.

HABITANT

- Cocktail glass
- Mixing glass
- 3/4 ounce gin
- 3/4 ounce sweet red vermouth
- 3/4 ounce maple syrup
- 2 dashes Angostura bitters

SPICY, SWEET SHORT DRINK FOR ANY TIME OF THE YEAR

Mix all the ingredients together firmly, with ice, in the mixing glass and strain into the cocktail glass.

BLUE DIAMOND

- Champagne glass or flute
- Shaker
- 3/4 ounce gin
- 3/4 ounce blue curaçao
- 3/4 ounce lemon juice
- Champagne or sparkling wine for topping up

GARNISH
- 1 maraschino cherry

FRUITY CHAMPAGNE COCKTAIL FOR A RECEPTION

Shake all the ingredients, except the champagne, together, with ice, in the shaker and strain into the champagne glass. Spear the cherry on a toothpick and add it to the glass.

GIN

BLACK GYPSY

- Cocktail glass
- Shaker
- 2/3 ounce gin
- 1/3 ounce mandarin-flavored liqueur
- 1/3 ounce lemon juice
- 5 drops of pastis

FRUITY, SHARP DRINK

Shake all the ingredients together, with ice, in the shaker and strain into the cocktail glass.

PIRATE

- Highball/Collins glass
- Shaker
- 1 1/2 ounces passion-fruit liqueur
- 1 ounce cherry heering
- 3/4 ounce gin
- 2 tsp. lemon juice
- Tonic water for topping up

GARNISH
- 1/2 slice of orange
- 2 maraschino cherries

FRUITY, MEDIUM-DRY DRINK

Shake all the ingredients, except the tonic water, together, with ice, in the shaker and strain into the highball glass over ice cubes. Top up with the tonic water. Spear both the slice of orange and the cherries on a long wooden skewer so it looks like a sail and put it in the glass. Serve with a stirrer.

BABY DOC

- Highball/Collins glass
- 3/4 ounce gin
- 3/4 ounce kiwi-fruit-flavored liqueur
- 3/4 ounce pineapple juice
- 1 tsp. peppermint-flavored liqueur
- Tonic water for topping up

GARNISH
- 1 orange peel spiral

FRUITY DRINK FOR A SUMMER PARTY

Mix all the ingredients together, with ice cubes, in the highball glass. Hang the orange peel spiral over the rim of the glass.

Black Gypsy

GIN

DASH MADNEY

REFRESHING DRINK FOR THE SUMMER

- Highball/Collins glass
- Mixing glass
- 1 ounce gin
- 1/2 ounce maraschino
- 1/2 ounce crème de banane
- Bitter lemon for topping up

GARNISH
- 1 maraschino cherry

Stir all the ingredients together, except the bitter lemon, with ice, in the mixing glass and strain into the highball glass over ice cubes. Top up with bitter lemon and stir well. Perch the cherry on the rim of the glass and serve the drink with a stirrer.

PERFECT GIN COCKTAIL

MEDIUM-DRY DRINK FOR THE EVENING

- Cocktail glass
- Mixing glass
- 1 1/2 ounces gin
- 2 tsp. dry vermouth
- 2 tsp. sweet red vermouth

Mix the ingredients together, with ice cubes, in the mixing glass and strain into the cocktail glass.

ALEXANDER'S SISTER

CREAMY, SWEET DRINK FOR THE AFTERNOON

- Cocktail glass
- Shaker
- 3/4 ounce gin
- 3/4 ounce crème de menthe
- 3/4 ounce light cream

Shake the ingredients together firmly, with ice, in the shaker and strain into the glass.

RESOLUTE

- Cocktail glass
- Shaker
- 3/4 ounce gin
- 2 tsp. apricot brandy
- 2 tsp. lemon juice

MEDIUM-DRY DRINK

Shake the ingredients together, with ice, in the shaker and strain into the cocktail glass.

GOLDEN DAWN

- Cocktail glass
- Shaker
- 1 ounce gin
- 3/4 ounce orange juice
- 2 tsp. lemon juice
- 1 tsp. apricot brandy
- 3 dashes grenadine

FRUITY DRINK FOR ANY TIME OF YEAR

Shake all the ingredients together, with ice cubes, in the shaker and strain into the cocktail glass.

YELLOW FINGER

- Cocktail glass
- Shaker
- 3/4 ounce gin
- 3/4 ounce blackberry brandy
- 2 tsp. banana-flavored liqueur
- 1 dash light cream

FRUITY, MILD DRINK FOR ANY TIME OF YEAR

Shake all the ingredients together firmly, with ice, in the shaker and strain into the cocktail glass.

GIN

FALLEN ANGEL

- Cocktail glass
- Shaker
- 1 1/2 ounces gin
- 3/4 ounce lemon juice
- 2 dashes green crème de menthe
- 1 dash Angostura bitters

VERY FRUITY, DRY APERITIF

Shake all the ingredients together, with plenty of ice, in the shaker and strain into the glass.

BLUE VELVET

- Cocktail glass
- Mixing glass
- 3/4 ounce gin
- 3/4 ounce curaçao
- 1/2 ounce dry vermouth

GARNISH
- 1 slice of star fruit

DRY DRINK FOR THE EVENING

Mix the ingredients together, with ice, in the mixing glass and strain into the cocktail glass. Finally, perch the slice of star fruit on the rim of the glass.

CARIN

- Cocktail glass
- Mixing glass
- 1 ounce gin
- 1/2 ounce Dubonnet
- 1/2 ounce mandarin-flavored liqueur
- Extra: 1 piece of lemon peel

SWEET AFTER-DINNER DRINK

Mix the ingredients together, with ice, in the mixing glass and strain into the cocktail glass. Squeeze the piece of lemon peel over the drink and add the peel to the glass.

Fallen Angel

GIN

MINE

FRUITY, REFRESHING APERITIF OR AFTER-DINNER DRINK

- Highball/Collins glass
- 1 ounce gin
- Orange juice for topping up
- 1/2 slice of orange
- 3/4 ounce Campari

Pour the gin into the highball glass over the ice and top up with orange juice. Place the slice of orange in the glass and pour the Campari on top of it. Do not stir. Serve with a long stirrer.

MONTE CARLO IMPERIAL

REFRESHING CHAMPAGNE COCKTAIL FOR A RECEPTION

- Champagne flute
- Shaker
- 3/4 ounce gin
- 2 tsp. white crème de menthe
- Champagne or sparkling wine for topping up

Shake the ingredients, except the champagne, together, with ice, in the shaker and strain into the champagne flute. Top up with champagne.

WEDDING BELLS

DRINK FOR ANY TIME OF DAY

- Cocktail glass
- Shaker
- 3/4 ounce gin
- 3/4 ounce Dubonnet
- 3/4 ounce orange juice
- 2 tsp. brandy

Shake the ingredients together, with ice, in the shaker and strain into the glass.

MY FAIR LADY

- Cocktail glass
- Shaker
- 1 ounce gin
- 2 tsp. orange juice
- 2 tsp. lemon juice
- 1 tsp. egg white
- 1 dash grenadine

GARNISH
- 1/2 slice of orange

DRY, SPICY DRINK FOR THE EVENING

Shake all the ingredients together, with ice, in the shaker and strain into the cocktail glass. Perch the slice of orange on the rim of the glass.

SILVER JUBILEE

- Cocktail glass
- Shaker
- 1 1/2 ounces gin
- 1 1/2 ounces light cream
- 3/4 ounce banana-flavored liqueur

GARNISH
- 1 slice of banana

SPICY, SWEET AFTER-DINNER DRINK

Shake all the ingredients together well, with ice, in the shaker and strain into the cocktail glass. Spear the slice of banana on a toothpick and add it to the glass.

ADMIRAL

- Champagne or cocktail glass
- Shaker
- 1 1/2 ounces gin
- 3/4 ounce cherry-flavored liqueur

GARNISH
- 1 maraschino cherry

FRUITY, SPICY DRINK FOR ANY TIME OF YEAR

Shake all the ingredients together, with ice cubes, in the shaker and strain into the glass. Perch the cherry on the rim of the glass.

WHITE LADY

- Cocktail glass
- Shaker
- 3/4 ounce gin
- 3/4 ounce Cointreau
- 3/4 ounce lemon juice

GARNISH
- 1 lemon peel spiral

AROMATIC APERITIF

Shake the ingredients together, with ice, in the shaker and strain into the cocktail glass. Add the lemon to the glass.

CONCA D'ORO

- Cocktail glass
- Mixing glass
- 1 1/2 ounces gin
- 2 tsp. cherry brandy
- 2 tsp. maraschino
- 2 tsp. white curaçao
- Extra: 1 piece of orange peel

SWEET AFTER-DINNER DRINK

Mix the ingredients together, with ice, in the mixing glass and strain into the cocktail glass. Squeeze the orange peel over the drink and add the peel to the glass.

BANANZAS

- Cocktail glass
- Shaker
- 3/4 ounce gin
- 1/2 ounce crème de banane
- 1/2 ounce Drambuie
- 1/2 ounce grapefruit juice

GARNISH
- 1 maraschino cherry

SWEET DRINK FOR A PARTY

Shake the ingredients together, with ice, in the shaker and strain into the cocktail glass. Add the cherry to the glass.

White Lady

GIN

MILLION DOLLAR

SWEET APERITIF

- Cocktail glass
- Shaker
- 1 ounce gin
- 1 ounce sweet red vermouth
- 1 tsp. grenadine
- 1 tsp. pineapple juice
- 1 tsp. egg white

Shake the ingredients together firmly, with ice, in the shaker and strain into the glass.

CASINO

DRY APERITIF

- Cocktail glass
- Mixing glass
- 1 1/2 ounces gin
- 2 tsp. maraschino
- 2 tsp. lemon juice
- 1 dash orange bitters

GARNISH
- 1 maraschino cherry

Shake the ingredients together, with plenty of ice, in the shaker and strain into the cocktail glass. Add the cherry to the glass.

EMPIRE

VERY ALCOHOLIC, AFTER-DINNER DRINK

- Cocktail glass
- Mixing glass
- 1 ounce gin
- 1/2 ounce Calvados
- 1/2 ounce apricot brandy

GARNISH
- 1 maraschino cherry

Mix the ingredients together, with plenty of ice, in the mixing glass and strain into the cocktail glass. Spear the cherry on a toothpick and add it to the glass.

FLAMINGO

SPICY, FRUITY APERITIF

- Cocktail glass
- Shaker
- 1¹/2 ounces gin
- ³/4 ounce apricot brandy
- ³/4 ounce lemon juice
- 2 dashes grenadine

Shake all the ingredients together, with ice, in the shaker and strain into the cocktail glass.

LADY DI

FRUITY, SPARKLING CHAMPAGNE COCKTAIL FOR A RECEPTION

- Champagne glass with a sugared rim
- Shaker
- ³/4 ounce gin
- 2 tsp. Benedictine
- 2 tsp. orange juice
- 1 tsp. grenadine
- 2 dashes orange bitters
- Champagne or dry sparkling wine for topping up

GARNISH
- ¹/2 slice of orange
- 1 maraschino cherry

Shake all the ingredients, except the champagne, together, with ice, in the shaker. Strain into the champagne glass with the sugared rim and top up with champagne. Spear the fruit on a toothpick and lay the garnish across the rim of the glass.

SUZY WONG

REFRESHING, FRUITY, MEDIUM-DRY CHAMPAGNE COCKTAIL FOR A RECEPTION

- Champagne glass with a sugared rim
- Shaker
- ³/4 ounce gin
- ³/4 ounce mandarin-flavored liqueur
- ³/4 ounce lemon juice
- Champagne or dry sparkling wine for topping up

GARNISH
- ¹/2 slice of orange

Shake all the ingredients, except the champagne, together, with ice, in the shaker. Strain into the champagne glass with the sugared rim and top up with champagne. Perch the slice of orange on the rim of the glass.

GIN

CLOVER CLUB

- Cocktail glass
- Shaker
- 1 1/2 ounces gin
- 1/2 ounce grenadine
- 1/2 ounce lemon juice
- 1 egg white

BITTERSWEET DRINK FOR THE EVENING

Shake all the ingredients together, with ice, in the shaker. Strain and pour into the glass.

EMERALD

- Cocktail glass
- Mixing glass
- 1 ounce gin
- 2 tsp. green Chartreuse
- 2 tsp. yellow Chartreuse

GARNISH
- 1 green olive, stuffed with pimiento

SPICY APERITIF

Mix the ingredients together well, with ice, in the mixing glass and strain into the cocktail glass. Add the olive to the glass.

ALCUDIA

- Cocktail glass
- Shaker
- 1/2 ounce banana-flavored liqueur
- 1/2 ounce Galliano
- 1/2 ounce grapefruit juice

GARNISH
- 1/4 slice of orange
- 1 maraschino cherry

FRUITY DRINK FOR THE SUMMER

Shake all the ingredients together, with ice, in the shaker and strain into the cocktail glass. Perch the slice of orange on the rim of the glass and fasten the cherry to it with a toothpick.

Clover Club

GIN

RED LION

FRUITY, DRY DRINK FOR THE EVENING

- Cocktail glass, with sugared rim
- Shaker
- 3/4 ounce gin
- 3/4 ounce Grand Marnier
- 2 tsp. orange juice
- 2 tsp. lemon juice

Shake the ingredients together, with ice, in the shaker and strain into the glass.

THEATER

MEDIUM-DRY, REFRESHING COCKTAIL FOR A RECEPTION

- Champagne glass or flute
- Shaker
- 3/4 ounce gin
- 3/4 ounce peach brandy
- 2 tsp. banana-flavored liqueur
- 2 tsp. pineapple juice
- 1 dash lemon juice
- Dry champagne or sparkling wine for topping up

GARNISH
- 1 strawberry
- 1 sprig of mint

Shake all the ingredients together, with ice, in the shaker and strain into the champagne glass. Top up with the champagne or sparkling wine. Spear the strawberry and sprig of mint on a toothpick and lay the garnish across the rim of the glass.

BLUE LADY

FRUITY, SWEET DRINK FOR THE EVENING

- Cocktail glass, with sugared rim
- Shaker
- 3/4 ounce gin
- 3/4 ounce blue curaçao
- 3/4 ounce lemon juice

Shake the ingredients together, with ice, in the shaker and strain into the sugared-rim glass.

MAYFAIR

- Cocktail glass
- Shaker
- 1 ounce gin
- 1 ounce orange juice
- 3 dashes apricot brandy

FRUITY APERITIF OR AFTER-DINNER DRINK

Shake the ingredients together, with ice, in the shaker and strain into the cocktail glass.

HAWAIIAN

- Cocktail glass
- Shaker
- 1 ounce gin
- 3/4 ounce orange juice
- 2 tsp. triple sec

FRUITY APERITIF

Shake the ingredients together, with plenty of ice, in the shaker and strain into the cocktail glass.

FLYING

- Champagne flute
- Shaker
- 3/4 ounce gin
- 3/4 ounce Cointreau
- 3/4 ounce lemon juice
- Champagne or dry sparkling wine for topping up

GARNISH

- 1 maraschino cherry

REFRESHING APERITIF OR AFTER-DINNER DRINK

Shake all the ingredients together, except the champagne, with plenty of ice, in the shaker and strain into the champagne flute. Top up, then add the cherry to the glass.

BRANDY-BASED DRINKS

BRANDY

ZOOM

SWEET AFTER-DINNER DRINK

- Cocktail glass
- Shaker
- 1 1/2 ounces brandy
- 3/4 ounce light cream
- 2 tsp. honey

Shake the ingredients together firmly, with ice, in the shaker and strain into the cocktail glass.

PIERRE COLLINS

REFRESHING COLLINS FOR ANY TIME OF THE DAY

- Highball/Collins glass
- 1 1/2 ounces brandy
- 3/4 ounce lemon juice
- 2 tsp. sugar syrup
- Soda water for topping up

GARNISH
- 1/2 slice of lemon
- 1 maraschino cherry

Stir together the brandy, lemon juice, and sugar syrup in the highball glass with ice. Top up with soda water and stir until the glass condenses. Put the fruit on the rim of the glass.

COGNAC COLLINS

DRY, FRUITY COLLINS FOR THE EVENING

- Highball/Collins glass
- 1 1/2 ounces cognac
- 3/4 ounce lemon juice
- 2 tsp. sugar
- Soda water for topping up
- Extra: 1 slice of lemon, 1/2 slice of orange, and 1 maraschino cherry

Stir the cognac, sugar, and lemon juice together in the highball glass, with ice cubes. Top up with soda water and stir briefly. Add the fruit to the glass.

EGG SOUR

- Highball/Collins glass
- Shaker
- 1 ounce brandy
- 3/4 ounce lemon juice
- 2 tsp. triple sec
- 2 tsp. sugar syrup
- 1 egg

GARNISH
- 1/2 slice of orange
- 1 maraschino cherry

NOURISHING SOUR FOR THE EVENING

Shake the ingredients together firmly, with ice, in the shaker and strain into the glass. Spear the slice of orange and the cherry on a toothpick and place across the rim of the glass.

COCO DE MARTINIQUE

- Highball/Collins glass
- Shaker
- 2 3/4 ounces orange juice
- 1 3/4 ounces cream of coconut
- 1 ounce Armagnac
- 1 ounce Benedictine

FRUITY, SWEET LONG DRINK FOR THE EVENING

Shake all the ingredients together firmly, with ice cubes, in the shaker and strain into the highball glass over crushed ice.

B AND B

- Cocktail glass
- 1 ounce brandy
- 1 ounce Benedictine

STRONG, SHORT AFTER-DINNER DRINK OR TO ACCOMPANY COFFEE

Mix the ingredients together in the cocktail glass. Add ice to taste.

BRANDY

ALEXANDER

CREAMY DRINK FOR THE EVENING

- Cocktail glass with a chocolate rim
- Shaker
- 3/4 ounce brandy or cognac
- 3/4 ounce brown crème de cacao
- 3/4 ounce light cream
- Extra: Grated nutmeg

GARNISH

- A chocolate stick

Shake all the ingredients together firmly, with ice, in the shaker and strain into the glass. Sprinkle with a little nutmeg and garnish with chocolate.

ECSTASY

AROMATIC, SHORT APERITIF

- Cocktail glass
- Mixing glass
- 3/4 ounce brandy
- 3/4 ounce Drambuie
- 3/4 ounce dry vermouth

Mix the ingredients together, with plenty of ice, in the mixing glass and strain into the cocktail glass.

LUMUMBA

SPICY DRINK FOR THE SUMMER

- Highball glass
- 1 1/2 ounces brandy
- Cold cocoa for topping up

GARNISH

- 1/2 ounce whipped cream
- Cocoa powder

Pour the brandy into the highball glass, top up with cocoa, and stir briefly. Heap whipped cream on top and dust with cocoa powder.

Alexander

BRANDY

JAMES

DELICATE, DRY, AFTER-DINNER DRINK

- Cocktail glass
- Mixing glass
- 3/4 ounce cognac
- 3/4 ounce gin
- 3/4 ounce yellow Chartreuse

GARNISH
- 1 green maraschino cherry

Mix all the ingredients together, with ice cubes, in the mixing glass and strain into the cocktail glass. Perch the cherry on the rim of the glass.

DAISY

FRUITY, ELEGANT, TANGY APERITIF

- Cocktail glass
- Mixing glass
- 1 ounce gin
- 3/4 ounce cognac
- 2 tsp. apricot brandy

GARNISH
- 1/2 slice of lemon

Stir all the ingredients together in the mixing glass, with ice cubes, and strain into the cocktail glass. Perch the slice of lemon on the edge of the glass.

PICASSO

TANGY, FRUITY DRINK FOR THE EVENING

- Cocktail glass
- Shaker
- 1 ounce cognac
- 3/4 ounce Dubonnet
- 2 tsp. lemon juice
- 4 dashes sugar syrup

Shake all the ingredients together firmly, with ice cubes, in the shaker and strain into the cocktail glass.

STINGER

- Cocktail glass
- Mixing glass
- 1 1/2 ounces brandy or cognac
- 3/4 ounce white crème de menthe

SPICY, FRESH AFTER-DINNER DRINK

Mix the ingredients together in the mixing glass, with ice, and strain into the cocktail glass.

RITZ

- Champagne flute
- Shaker
- 3/4 ounce brandy or cognac
- 3/4 ounce Cointreau
- 3/4 ounce orange juice
- Champagne or sparkling wine for topping up

GARNISH
- 1/2 slice of orange

AROMATIC CHAMPAGNE COCKTAIL TO SERVE AS AN APERITIF OR AFTER-DINNER DRINK

Shake all the ingredients, except the champagne, together, with ice, in the shaker and strain into the glass. Top up with champagne or sparkling wine. Perch the slice of orange on the rim of the glass.

GREEN DRAGON

- Cocktail glass
- Shaker
- 1 1/2 ounces cognac
- 2 tsp. green crème de menthe

FRESH, SPICY AFTER-DINNER DRINK

Shake the cognac and liqueur together well, with ice cubes, in the shaker and strain into the glass.

BRANDY

SIDECAR

- Cocktail glass
- Shaker
- 3/4 ounce brandy or cognac
- 3/4 ounce Cointreau
- 3/4 ounce lemon juice

SHARP-TASTING APERITIF

Shake the ingredients together, with ice, in the shaker and strain into the cocktail glass.

PANAMAC

- Cocktail glass
- Shaker
- 3/4 ounce cognac or brandy
- 3/4 ounce brown crème de cacao
- 3/4 ounce light cream
- Extra: Grated nutmeg

CREAMY DRINK FOR THE EVENING

Shake all the ingredients together firmly, with ice, in the shaker and strain into the cocktail glass. Sprinkle with a little nutmeg.

MOONLIGHT

- Cocktail glass
- Mixing glass
- 1/2 ounce light cream
- 2 tsp. cognac
- 2 tsp. mandarin-flavored liqueur
- 2 tsp. sugar syrup
- 5 tsp. cold black coffee
- Extra: 1 piece of mandarin peel and 1 orange peel spiral

CREAMY, SWEET AFTER-DINNER DRINK

Mix all the ingredients together, except the coffee and cream, with ice, in the mixing glass and strain into the glass. Add the coffee, stir, and float the cream on top. Squeeze the mandarin peel into the drink. Hang the spiral of orange peel over the edge of the drink.

Sidecar

BRANDY

QUEEN MARY

ELEGANT, SWEET APERITIF OR AFTER-DINNER DRINK

- Cocktail glass
- Shaker
- 1 ounce cognac
- 1 ounce Cointreau
- 1 dash anisette
- 1 dash grenadine

GARNISH
- 1 maraschino cherry

Shake all the ingredients together, with ice, in the shaker and strain into the cocktail glass. Perch the cherry on the rim of the glass.

SARATOGA

TANGY APERITIF

- Cocktail glass
- Mixing glass
- 1½ ounces brandy
- 2 dashes Angostura bitters
- 2 dashes maraschino

Mix the ingredients together, with ice, in the mixing glass and strain into the cocktail glass.

ALBA

FRUITY, ELEGANT, TANGY DRINK FOR THE EVENING

- Cocktail glass
- Shaker
- 1½ ounces cognac
- 3/4 ounce orange juice
- 2 tsp. raspberry cordial

GARNISH
- ½ slice of orange

Shake all the ingredients together, with ice cubes, in the shaker and strain into the chilled cocktail glass. Perch the slice of orange on the rim of the glass.

GLORIA

DRY APERITIF

- Cocktail glass
- Mixing glass
- 1/2 ounce brandy
- 1/2 ounce scotch
- 1/2 ounce Campari
- 2 tsp. vermouth
- 2 tsp. amaretto

GARNISH
- 1 piece of lemon peel
- 1 green maraschino cherry

Stir the ingredients together in the mixing glass, with ice, and strain into the cocktail glass. Spear the lemon peel and cherry on a toothpick and lay the garnish across the rim of the glass.

AMERICAN SEA

FRUITY, REFINED, DRY APERITIF

- Cocktail glass
- Shaker
- 1 ounce orange juice
- 3/4 ounce cognac
- 3/4 ounce dry vermouth
- 2 tsp. white crème de menthe

Shake all the ingredients together firmly, with ice cubes, in the shaker and strain into the cocktail glass.

BRANDY COCKTAIL

DELICATE, DRY COCKTAIL FOR THE EVENING

- Cocktail glass
- Mixing glass
- 1 1/2 ounces brandy
- 1 tsp. sugar syrup
- 3 dashes Angostura bitters

GARNISH
- 1 green maraschino cherry

Stir all the ingredients together in the mixing glass, with ice, and strain into the cocktail glass. Perch the cherry on the rim of the glass.

BRANDY

AMERICAN BEAUTY

STRONG, SHARP DRINK

- Goblet
- Shaker
- 1 ounce brandy
- 1 ounce dry vermouth
- 1 ounce white crème de menthe
- 1 ounce orange juice
- 1/2 ounce port

Shake all the ingredients together, except the port, in the shaker, with ice, and strain into the goblet. Slowly pour in the port and stir.

EAST INDIA

FRUITY APERITIF

- Cocktail shaker
- Shaker
- 1 ounce brandy
- 3/4 ounce pineapple juice
- 2 tsp. orange curaçao
- 1 dash Angostura bitters

GARNISH
- 1 maraschino cherry

Shake the ingredients together, with plenty of ice, in the shaker and strain into the cocktail glass. Drop the cherry into the glass.

QUEEN ELIZABETH

MEDIUM-DRY APERITIF

- Cocktail glass
- Mixing glass
- 3/4 ounce brandy
- 3/4 ounce sweet red vermouth
- 1 tsp. triple sec

Stir the ingredients together, with ice, in the mixing glass and strain into the cocktail glass.

American Beauty

BRANDY

NEW ORLEANS SIDECAR

ELEGANT, DRY DRINK FOR PARTIES

- Cocktail glass
- Shaker
- 3/4 ounce brandy
- 3/4 ounce light rum
- 3/4 ounce lemon juice
- 2 tsp. triple sec
- 1 dash pastis
- 1 dash grenadine

Shake all the ingredients together firmly, with ice cubes, in the cocktail shaker and strain into the cocktail glass.

CHÂTEAU SARRE

AROMATIC DRINK FOR PARTIES

- Cocktail glass
- Shaker
- 1 1/2 ounces brandy
- 1/2 ounce crème de banane
- 1/2 ounce maraschino

GARNISH
- 1 maraschino cherry

Shake all the ingredients together, with ice, in the shaker and strain into the cocktail glass. Put the cherry in the glass.

BERMUDA HIGHBALL

SPICY, MILD DRINK FOR THE EVENING

- Highball/Collins glass
- Mixing glass
- 1 ounce brandy
- 3/4 ounce gin
- 1 dash orange bitters
- Ginger ale for topping up
- Extra: 1 kumquat

Stir together the brandy, gin, and orange bitters in the mixing glass, with ice, and strain into the glass. Top up with ginger ale and add the kumquat to the glass.

BRANDY EGGNOG

- Rocks glass
- Shaker
- 3 1/2 ounces milk
- 1 1/2 ounces brandy
- 2 tsp. sugar syrup
- 1 egg yolk
- Extra: Grated nutmeg

NOURISHING EGGNOG FOR THE AFTERNOON

Shake the ingredients together firmly, with ice, in the shaker and strain into the glass. Sprinkle with nutmeg.

COGNAC CASSIS

- Cocktail glass
- Shaker
- 1 ounce cognac
- 1 ounce crème de cassis

FRUITY, SWEET DRINK FOR THE EVENING

Shake the cognac and crème de cassis together, with ice, in the shaker and strain into the cocktail glass.

COGNAC FLIP

- Cocktail glass
- Shaker
- 2 ounces cognac
- 1 egg yolk
- 2 tbsp. sugar

DELICATE, TANGY FLIP FOR THE EVENING

Shake all the ingredients together firmly and briefly in the shaker and strain into the cocktail glass.

BRANDY

BETWEEN THE SHEETS

- Cocktail glass
- Shaker
- 3/4 ounce cognac
- 3/4 ounce light rum
- 3/4 ounce Cointreau
- 1 dash lemon juice

TANGY, FRUITY SHORT DRINK FOR THE EVENING

Shake all the ingredients together, with ice, in the shaker and strain into the cocktail glass.

CORONADO

- Cocktail glass
- Shaker
- 3/4 ounce light cream
- 1/2 ounce crème de banane
- 1/2 ounce peach-flavored liqueur
- 2 tsp. brandy

GARNISH
- 1 chocolate cookie
- Grated chocolate

CREAMY, SWEET AFTER-DINNER DRINK

Shake the ingredients together firmly, with ice, in the shaker and strain into the cocktail glass. Garnish the drink with the cookie and a little grated chocolate.

HONEYMOON

- Cocktail glass
- Mixing glass
- 1 1/2 ounces cognac
- 2 tsp. Cointreau
- 2 tsp. white wine

GARNISH
- 1 slice of orange

FRUITY, DELICATELY DRY COCKTAIL FOR THE EVENING

Stir the ingredients together in the mixing glass, with ice, and strain into the cocktail glass. Perch the slice of orange on the rim of the glass.

Between the Sheets

BRANDY

WILLEM VON ORANIEN

SLIGHTLY BITTER APERITIF

- Cocktail glass
- Mixing glass
- 3/4 ounce brandy
- 2 tsp. triple sec
- 2 tsp. orange bitters
- Extra: 1 piece of orange peel

Mix the ingredients together in the mixing glass, with ice, and strain into the cocktail glass. Squeeze the orange peel over the drink.

GREEN LOVE

FRUITY, BITTERSWEET DRINK FOR THE EVENING

- Cocktail glass
- Shaker
- 3/4 ounce cognac
- 3/4 ounce blue curaçao
- 3/4 ounce mandarin-flavored liqueur
- 3/4 lemon juice

GARNISH
- 1 slice of lemon

Shake all the ingredients together firmly, with ice cubes, in the shaker and strain into the cocktail glass. Put the slice of lemon on the rim of the glass.

HORSE'S NECK

REFRESHING LONG DRINK FOR ANY OCCASION

- Highball/Collins glass
- 1 1/2 ounces brandy
- 1 dash Angostura bitters
- Ginger ale for topping up

GARNISH
- 1 lemon peel spiral

Pour the brandy and Angostura bitters into the highball glass with some ice. Top up with ginger ale and stir. Hang the lemon peel spiral over the edge of the glass and serve the drink with a stirrer.

BRANDY COLA

SWEET, LONG DRINK FOR THE EVENING

- Highball/Collins glass
- 1 1/2 ounces brandy
- Cola for topping up

GARNISH

- 1/2 slice of lemon

Pour the brandy into the highball glass, with ice cubes. Top up with cola and stir briefly. Add the slice of lemon to the glass.

BREAKFAST EGGNOG

SWEET EGGNOG FOR ANY TIME OF THE YEAR

- Highball/Collins glass
- Shaker
- 1 1/2 ounces cognac
- 3/4 ounce white curaçao
- 1/2 ounce sugar syrup
- 1 egg
- Milk for topping up

Shake all the ingredients, except the milk, together, with ice, in the shaker and strain into the glass. Top up with milk and stir.

LADY BE GOOD

MEDIUM-DRY APERITIF

- Cocktail glass
- Shaker
- 3/4 ounce brandy
- 3/4 ounce dry vermouth
- 3/4 ounce orange juice
- 1 tsp. white crème de menthe
- 1 tsp. grenadine

Shake the ingredients together, with ice, in the shaker and strain into the glass.

BRANDY

FIRST NIGHT

SMOOTH, CREAMY DRINK

- Cocktail glass
- Shaker
- 1 ounce brandy
- 1/2 ounce Benedictine
- 1/2 ounce coffee-flavored liqueur
- 1 tsp. whipping cream

Put the brandy, Benedictine, cream and coffee-flavored liqueur in a shaker with plenty of ice. Shake and strain into a cocktail glass.

FAR WEST

MILD, SPICY DRINK FOR THE EVENING

- Cocktail glass
- Shaker
- 3/4 ounce cognac
- 3/4 ounce advocaat
- 3/4 ounce sweet white vermouth
- Extra: Ground cinnamon

Shake all the ingredients together firmly, with ice cubes, in the shaker and strain into the cocktail glass. Sprinkle with a pinch of cinnamon.

ROLLS ROYCE

FRUITY APERITIF

- Cocktail glass
- Shaker
- 3/4 ounce brandy
- 3/4 ounce Cointreau
- 3/4 ounce orange juice

Shake the ingredients together, with ice, in the shaker and strain into the cocktail glass.

First Night

BRANDY

SALAMANDER ZOOM

SWEET AFTER-DINNER DRINK

- Cocktail glass
- Shaker
- 1 1/2 ounces brandy
- 3/4 ounce light cream
- 2 tsp. brown sugar

Shake all the ingredients together, with ice cubes, in the shaker and strain into the cocktail glass.

NIKOLASCHKA

SPICY DRINK FOR THE AFTERNOON

- Pousee-café glass
- 3/4 ounce brandy or cognac
- 1 slice of lemon, peeled
- 1 tsp. sugar
- 1 tsp. ground coffee

Put the brandy in the glass, place the slice of lemon on the rim of the glass, and sprinkle one half with sugar and the other with ground coffee.

B AND P

ELEGANT, TANGY DRINK FOR THE EVENING

- Rocks glass
- 3/4 ounce brandy
- 3/4 ounce port

Stir the ingredients together in the glass with ice cubes.

OLYMPIC

- Cocktail glass
- Shaker
- 3/4 ounce brandy or cognac
- 3/4 ounce triple sec
- 3/4 ounce orange juice

MEDIUM-DRY, FRUITY APERITIF OR AFTER-DINNER DRINK

Shake the ingredients together, with ice, in the shaker and strain into the glass.

PISCO SOUR

- Rocks glass with sugared rim
- Shaker
- 1 1/2 ounces pisco
- 3/4 ounce lemon juice
- 1 tsp. sugar
GARNISH
- 1 slice of lemon
- 1 maraschino cherry

REFRESHING, SHARP SHORT DRINK FOR PARTIES

Shake all the ingredients together, with ice, in the shaker and strain into the glass with the sugared rim. Perch the fruit on the rim of the glass.

PRINCE OF WALES

- Silver goblet or highball/Collins glass
- 3/4 ounce brandy or cognac
- 2 tsp. orange curaçao
- 1 dash Angostura bitters
- Champagne or sparkling wine for topping up
- Extra: 1/2 slice of orange, 1/2 slice of lemon, and 2 maraschino cherries

AROMATIC CHAMPAGNE COCKTAIL FOR THE EVENING

Mix all the ingredients together in the goblet or glass, with ice. Put the fruit in the glass. Serve the drink with a stirrer.

BRANDY

CHERRY BLOSSOM

- Cocktail glass
- Shaker
- 3/4 ounce cognac
- 3/4 ounce cherry brandy
- 3/4 ounce lemon juice
- 2 tsp. Cointreau
- 2 tsp. grenadine

REFINED, DRY DRINK

Shake all the ingredients together firmly, with ice cubes, in the shaker and strain in the glass.

IBU

- Champagne flute
- Shaker
- 3/4 ounce brandy
- 3/4 ounce apricot brandy
- 3/4 ounce orange juice
- Champagne or dry sparkling wine for topping up

GARNISH
- 1/2 slice of orange

REFRESHING CHAMPAGNE COCKTAIL FOR THE EVENING

Shake all the ingredients, except the champagne or sparkling wine, together in the shaker, with ice, and strain into the glass. Top up with champagne and perch the orange on the rim of the glass.

RED MOON

- Champagne glass or flute
- Shaker
- 3/4 ounce brandy or cognac
- 3/4 ounce passion-fruit juice
- 2 tsp. strawberry syrup
- Champagne or sparkling wine for topping up

GARNISH
- 1 maraschino cherry

SWEETISH, FRUITY CHAMPAGNE COCKTAIL FOR A RECEPTION

Shake all the ingredients, except the champagne or sparkling wine, together, with ice, in the shaker. Strain into the champagne glass and top up with champagne or sparkling wine. Spear the cherry on a toothpick and add it to the glass.

Cherry Blossom

BRANDY

BRANDY FLIP

- Champagne flute
- Shaker
- 1 1/2 ounces brandy
- 1 tsp. sugar syrup
- 1 egg yolk
- Extra: Grated nutmeg

CREAMY FLIP FOR THE AFTERNOON

Shake all the ingredients together firmly, with ice, in the shaker and strain into the glass. Sprinkle with a little nutmeg.

FRENCH CONNECTION

- Rocks glass
- 1 ounce cognac
- 3/4 ounce amaretto

BITTERSWEET AFTER-DINNER DRINK

Stir the cognac and amaretto together in the glass with ice cubes.

AMERICAN ROSE

- Wine glass
- Shaker
- 1 1/2 ounces brandy
- 1 tsp. grenadine
- 1/2 fresh peach, peeled and mashed
- 1/2 tsp. Pernod
- Champagne or sparkling wine
GARNISH
- Small wedge of fresh peach

FRUITY, REFRESHING COCKTAIL

Mix all ingredients, except the champagne, in the shaker. Shake firmly and pour into the wine glass. Top up with champagne and garnish with peach wedge.

CHARLES

BITTER, SHORT APERITIF

- Cocktail glass
- Mixing glass
- 2 ounces brandy
- 1/2 ounce sweet vermouth
- 2–3 dashes Angostura bitters

Combine all ingredients in the mixing glass, with ice cubes, and stir. Strain into chilled cocktail glass.

CHICAGO

REFRESHING, SPARKLING COCKTAIL

- Wine glass with sugared rim
- Mixing glass
- 2 ounces brandy
- 1 dash triple sec
- 1 dash Angostura bitters
- Champagne or sparkling wine

GARNISH
- Lemon wedge

Mix brandy, triple sec, and bitters, with cracked ice, in a mixing glass and strain into wine glass. Fill with champagne and garnish with lemon.

MARCONI WIRELESS

SWEET, FRUITY DRINK

- Cocktail glass
- Shaker
- 3 ounces apple brandy
- 1/2 ounce sweet vermouth
- 3-5 dashes orange bitters

Combine all ingredients, with ice, in the shaker. Shake well and strain into glass.

BRANDY

GOLDEN GLEEM

FRUITY, FRESH COCKTAIL

- Wine glass
- Shaker
- 1 ounce brandy
- 1 ounce Grand Marnier
- 1/2 ounce lemon juice
- 1/2 ounce orange juice
GARNISH
- Orange or lemon peel to decorate

Shake the ingredients together, with ice, in a shaker and strain into a wine glass.

PANAMA

SHORT APERITIF

- Cocktail glass
- Shaker
- 2 ounces brandy
- 1 1/2 ounces white crème de cacao
- 1 1/2 ounces half-and-half

Shake the ingredients together, with ice, in a shaker and strain into a cocktail glass.

POOP DECK

DRY, FRUITY COCKTAIL

- Cocktail glass
- Shaker
- 2 ounces brandy
- 1 ounce ruby port
- 1/2 ounce blackberry brandy

Shake the ingredients together, with ice, in a shaker and strain into a cocktail glass.

Golden Gleem

BRANDY

SLEEPY HEAD

HERBY, REFRESHING DRINK

- Highball/Collins glass
- 3 ounces brandy
- 5 mint leaves
- Ginger ale

GARNISH
- Orange twist

Lightly muddle mint leaves with brandy in the bottom of a chilled glass. Fill with ice cubes and ginger ale. Stir gently and garnish with the orange twist.

STIRRUP CUP

SWEET, FRUITY DRINK

- Rocks glass
- Shaker
- 2 ounces brandy
- 1 1/2 ounces cherry brandy
- 1 1/2 ounces lemon juice
- 1 tsp. sugar

Shake all the ingredients together, with ice, in the shaker and strain into the glass over ice cubes.

THUNDER

SPICY, AROMATIC DRINK

- Cocktail glass
- Shaker
- 2 ounces brandy
- 1 tsp. sugar
- 1/4 tsp. cayenne pepper
- 1 egg yolk

Combine ingredients with cracked ice in the shaker. Shake vigorously and pour into glass.

VIA VENETO

- Rocks glass
- Shaker
- 2 ounces brandy
- 1 ounce Sambuca
- 1 ounce lemon juice
- 1/2 tsp. sugar
- 1 egg white

STRONG, SHARP DRINK

Shake all the ingredients, with ice, in the shaker and pour into glass.

YELLOW PARROT

- Cocktail glass
- Shaker
- 2 ounces brandy
- 2 ounces Pernod
- 2 ounces Chartreuse

AROMATIC APERITIF

Shake all the ingredients, with ice, in the shaker and pour into glass.

MONTANA

- Rocks glass
- Mixing glass
- 2 ounces brandy
- 1 ounce ruby port
- 1 ounce dry vermouth
- 1 dash Angostura bitters

DRY, BITTER COCKTAIL

Shake all the ingredients, with ice, in the mixing glass and strain into glass.

BRANDY

WHIP

- Cocktail glass
- Shaker
- 1 ounce brandy
- 1 ounce pastis
- 1 ounce dry vermouth
- 1 ounce curaçao

SOPHISTICATED, HERBY DRINK

Shake all the ingredients, with ice, in the shaker and strain into glass.

NETHERLANDS

- Rocks glass
- Shaker
- 2 ounces brandy
- 1 ounce white curaçao
- 1 dash orange bitters

BITTER, SHORT DRINK

Shake all the ingredients, with ice, in the shaker and strain into glass, over ice cubes.

POLONAISE

- Rocks glass
- Shaker
- 2 ounces brandy
- 1/2 ounce blackberry brandy
- 1/2 ounce dry sherry
- 3 dashes lemon juice
- 1 dash of orange bitters

BITTER, FRUITY DRINK

Shake all the ingredients, with ice, in the shaker and strain into glass, over ice cubes.

Whip

BRANDY

APPLE BLOSSOM

FRUITY, SHARP DRINK

- Rocks glass
- Mixing glass
- 2 ounces brandy
- 1 1/2 ounces apple juice
- 1 tsp. lemon juice

GARNISH
- Lemon slice

Combine all ingredients in mixing glass and stir well. Pour into glass over ice cubes. Garnish with lemon.

COLD DECK

ZESTY, STRONG DRINK

- Cocktail glass
- Shaker
- 2 ounces brandy
- 1/2 ounce sweet vermouth
- 1/2 ounce white crème de menthe

Shake all the ingredients, with ice, in the shaker and strain into glass.

PRAIRIE OYSTER WITH A KICK

SPICY, TASTY COCKTAIL

- Rocks glass
- Shaker
- 2 ounces brandy
- 1/2 ounce red wine vinegar
- 1/2 ounce Worcestershire sauce
- 1 tsp. tomato catsup
- 1 dash Tabasco sauce
- Cayenne pepper to taste
- 1 egg yolk

Combine all ingredients, except the cayenne and egg, in the shaker, with ice. Strain into glass. Float egg on top of drink and sprinkle with cayenne. Swallow in one swig without breaking the yolk.

DEAUVILLE

- Cocktail glass
- Shaker
- 1 1/2 ounces brandy
- 1 ounce Calvados
- 1/2 ounce Cointreau
- 1/2 ounce lemon juice

FRUITY, SHARP DRINK

Shake all the ingredients, with ice, in the shaker and strain into glass.

FANTASIO

- Cocktail glass
- Mixing glass
- 2 ounces brandy
- 1 ounce vermouth
- 2 tsp. maraschino liqueur
- 2 tsp. white crème de menthe

DRY, STRONG COCKTAIL

Combine all ingredients with cracked ice in a mixing glass and stir well. Strain into chilled cocktail glass.

FJORD

- Cocktail glass
- Shaker
- 2 ounces brandy
- 1 ounce Aquavit
- 2 ounces orange juice
- 1 ounce lime juice
- 2 tsp. grenadine

SHARP, FRUITY DRINK

Shake all the ingredients, with ice, in the shaker and strain into glass.

BRANDY

Ross Royale

- Cocktail glass
- Shaker
- 1 ounce brandy
- 1 ounce crème de banane
- 1 ounce mint chocolate liqueur
- ice cubes

RICH, CREAMY DRINK

Shake all the ingredients, with ice, in the shaker and strain into glass.

METROPOLITAN

- Cocktail glass
- Shaker
- 2 ounces brandy
- 1 ounce sweet vermouth
- 1 dash Angostura bitters

GARNISH
- 1 maraschino cherry

A WARM, EVENING APERITIF

Coat the glass with the bitters. Shake the brandy and vermouth with cracked ice. Strain and pour.

HAUTE COUTURE

- Cocktail glass
- Mixing glass
- 3/4 ounce brandy
- 3/4 ounce Benedictine
- 3/4 ounce brown crème de cacao

STRONG, SHORT AFTER-DINNER DRINK

Stir all the ingredients together in the mixing glass, with ice, and strain into the cocktail glass.

Ross Royale

CHAMPAGNE
ND WINE-BASED DRINKS

CHAMPAGNE

OHIO I

- Cocktail glass
- Mixing glass
- 3/4 ounce Canadian whiskey
- 2 tsp. sweet red vermouth
- 1 dash Angostura bitters
- Sparkling wine or champagne for topping up

SPICY APERITIF

Mix the whiskey, vermouth, Angostura bitters together, with ice, in the mixing glass and strain into the cocktail glass. Top up with the sparkling wine.

OHIO II

- Champagne glass
- 3/4 ounce Cointreau
- 3/4 ounce brandy
- 1 dash Angostura bitters
- Sparkling wine or champagne for topping up
GARNISH
- 1 maraschino cherry

AROMATIC COCKTAIL FOR A PARTY

Thoroughly mix the Cointreau, brandy, and bitters in the champagne glass. Add two small ice cubes and top up with sparkling wine. Perch the cherry on the rim of the glass.

STRAWBERRY FIELDS

- Champagne glass
- 5 strawberries, diced
- 1 tsp. orange-flavored liqueur
- Pink sparkling wine or champagne for topping up

FRUITY, PINK APERITIF

Put the diced strawberries in the glass. Pour the liqueur over them and top up with sparkling wine. Serve with a teaspoon.

KIR IMPERIAL I

FRUITY CHAMPAGNE COCKTAIL FOR A RECEPTION

- Champagne flute
- 2 tsp. raspberry-flavored liqueur
- 3¹/₂ ounces champagne or sparkling wine for topping up

Pour the liqueur into the glass and top up with the champagne or wine.

KIR IMPERIAL II

SWEET CHAMPAGNE APERITIF

- Champagne flute
- Shaker
- ³/4 ounce crème de cassis
- ³/4 ounce vodka
- Champagne for topping up

Shake the crème de cassis and vodka together, with ice, in the shaker and strain into the glass. Top up with champagne.

ORANGE CHAMPAGNE

FRUITY COCKTAIL FOR A PARTY

- Champagne flute
- ³/4 ounce orange curaçao
- Sparkling wine or champagne for topping up
GARNISH
- I orange peel spiral

Pour the curaçao into the champagne flute, top up with sparkling wine or champagne, and hang over the rim of the glass.

CHAMPAGNE

RITZ FIZZ

- Champagne flute
- 1 sugar cube
- 3–4 dashes Angostura bitters
- 1/2 ounce brandy or cognac
- Champagne for topping up

DRY DRINK FOR A CELEBRATION

Put the sugar lump in the flute and add the bitters to soak into the sugar. Add the brandy, then top up with champagne.

APRICOT CHAMPAGNE

- Champagne glass
- Mixing glass
- 3/4 apricot brandy
- 1 ounce light rum
- Champagne for topping up

FRUITY COCKTAIL FOR HOT DAYS

Mix the apricot brandy and rum together, with ice, in the mixing glass and strain into the champagne glass. Top up with champagne.

FRANÇOIS BISE

- Champagne flute
- 1 tsp. raspberry purée
- Champagne for topping up

FRUITY CHAMPAGNE APERITIF

Put the raspberry purée into the glass and top up with champagne.

Ritz Fizz

CHAMPAGNE

LILA CRYSTAL

LIGHT COCKTAIL FOR A RECEPTION

- Champagne glass
- Mixing glass
- 3/4 ounce Benedictine
- 2 tsp. gin
- 2 dashes orange bitters
- Dry sparkling wine or champagne for topping up
- 1 piece of orange peel

GARNISH
- 1 maraschino cherry

Mix the Benedictine, gin, and orange bitters together in the mixing glass and strain into the glass. Top up with champagne or wine. Squeeze the orange peel over the drink and add the maraschino cherry to the glass.

CHAMPAGNE FLIP

FRUITY DRINK FOR THE EVENING

- Champagne flute
- Shaker
- 1 1/2 ounces port
- 1 egg yolk
- 1 tsp. sugar
- Sparkling wine or champagne for topping up

Shake the port, egg yolk, and sugar together, with ice, in the shaker and strain into the glass. Top up with the sparkling wine.

CHAMPAGNE COBBLER

FRUITY, MILD DRINK FOR A SUMMER PARTY

- Cocktail glass
- 3/4 ounce maraschino
- 3/4 ounce triple sec
- 2 tsp. lemon juice
- 1 peach half, diced
- 2 maraschino cherries
- 2 grapes
- Sparkling wine or champagne for topping up

Fill the cocktail glass one-third full with crushed ice. Mix the maraschino, triple sec, and lemon juice together in the cocktail glass. Add the fruit to the glass, top up with sparkling wine, and serve with a spoon.

EROTICA

FRUITY, REFRESHING APERITIF

- Champagne glass
- Shaker
- 3/4 ounce passion-fruit flavored liqueur
- 3/4 ounce vodka
- 3/4 ounce pineapple juice
- 1 dash Angostura bitters
- Dry sparkling wine or champagne for topping up
GARNISH
- 1 piece of pineapple
- 2 maraschino cherries

Shake all the ingredients, except the champagne, together, with ice, in the shaker. Strain into a champagne glass and top up with sparkling wine. Perch the piece of pineapple on the rim of the glass and fasten the cherry to it using a toothpick.

HANSEATIC

FRUITY, ALCOHOLIC COCKTAIL FOR THE EVENING

- Champagne glass
- Shaker
- 3/4 ounce bourbon
- 3/4 ounce brandy
- 3/4 ounce blackberry-flavored liqueur
- Sparkling wine or champagne for topping up
GARNISH
- 1 slice of lemon

Shake all the ingredients together, except the sparkling wine, together, with ice, in the shaker and strain into the glass. Top up with sparkling wine. Perch the slice of lemon on the rim of the glass.

CHAMPAGNE DAISY

FRUITY CHAMPAGNE COCKTAIL FOR A PARTY

- Champagne flute
- Shaker
- 2 tsp. grenadine
- 2 tsp. lemon juice
- 3/4 ounce yellow Chartreuse
- Sparkling wine or champagne for topping up
GARNISH
- 1 strawberry

Shake the grenadine, lemon juice, and Chartreuse together, with ice cubes, in the shaker and strain into the champagne flute. Top up with sparkling wine. Perch the strawberry on the rim of the glass and serve the cocktail immediately.

CHAMPAGNE

CHAMPAGNE COCKTAIL I

- Champagne glass
- 1 sugar cube
- 2 dashes Angostura bitters
- Dry champagne or sparkling wine for topping up
- Extra: 1 piece of lemon peel (optional)

BITTERSWEET CHAMPAGNE COCKTAIL

Put the sugar cube into the champagne glass and soak it into the Angostura bitters. Top up with champagne or wine. Squeeze the lemon peel over the drink and add the peel to the glass.

CHAMPAGNE COCKTAIL II

- Champagne flute
- 1 sugar cube
- 1 dash Angostura bitters
- 3/4 ounce cognac
- Champagne for topping up
GARNISH
- 1 orange peel spiral

BITTERSWEET CHAMPAGNE COCKTAIL FOR THE EVENING

Put the sugar in the glass and soak it in the Angostura bitters. Add the cognac and top up with champagne. Hang the orange peel spiral over the rim of the glass.

MARGARET ROSE

- Champagne flute
- 3/4 ounce Campari
- Sparkling wine or champagne for topping up

SLIGHTLY BITTER APERITIF

Pour the Campari into the champagne flute and slowly top up with the sparkling wine.

Champagne Cocktail I

CHAMPAGNE

HARRY'S PICK-ME-UP

- Champagne flute
- Shaker
- 1 ounce cognac
- 2 tsp. lemon juice
- 2 dashes grenadine
- Sparkling wine or champagne for topping up

FRUITY, DELICATE TANGY COCKTAIL FOR A PARTY OR AS A PICK-ME-UP

Shake the cognac, lemon juice, and grenadine together, with ice, in the shaker and strain into the champagne flute. Top up with sparkling wine.

AMERICAN GLORY

- Champagne flute
- 1 1/2 ounces orange juice
- 3/4 ounce grenadine
- 2 tsp. lemon juice
- Sparkling wine or champagne for topping up
GARNISH
- 1 slice of orange

FRUITY, MILD APERITIF

Fill the champagne flute one-third full with crushed ice. Add the orange juice, grenadine, and lemon juice and mix well. Top up with sparkling wine. Perch the slice of orange on the rim of the glass.

NORTHERN LIGHT

- Champagne flute
- Shaker
- 3/4 ounce light rum
- 3/4 ounce triple sec
- Sparkling wine or champagne for topping up
- 1 piece of orange peel
GARNISH
- 1/2 slice of orange

AROMATIC COCKTAIL FOR A PARTY

Shake the rum and triple sec together, with ice, in the shaker and strain into the glass. Top up with sparkling wine and squeeze the orange peel over the drink. Perch the slice of orange on the rim of the glass.

ADRIA LOOK

FRUITY COCKTAIL FOR A SUMMER PARTY

- Champagne glass
- Mixing glass
- 3/4 ounce gin
- 3/4 ounce blue curaçao
- 2 tsp. lemon juice
- Sparkling wine or champagne for topping up
GARNISH
- 1 maraschino cherry
- 1/2 apricot

Mix the gin, curaçao, and lemon juice together, with ice, in the mixing glass and strain into the champagne glass. Top up with sparkling wine. Perch the fruit on the rim of the glass.

JAMES BOND

SLIGHTLY BITTER COCKTAIL FOR A PARTY

- Champagne glass
- 1 1/2 ounce vodka
- 1 dash Angostura bitters
- Sparkling wine or champagne for topping up

Thoroughly mix the vodka and Angostura bitters in the champagne glass. Top up with the sparkling wine.

BLUE SPLASH

FRUITY, SPARKLING DRINK FOR A PARTY

- Large rocks glass
- Mixing glass
- 3/4 ounce gin
- 3/4 ounce blue curaçao
- 3/4 ounce lemon juice
- 2 tsp. dry vermouth
- 1 dash Angostura bitters
- Sparkling wine or champagne for topping up
GARNISH
- 1 slice of orange

Mix all the ingredients, except the sparkling wine, together, with ice, in the mixing glass and strain into the glass. Top up with sparkling wine. Perch the slice of orange on the rim of the glass.

CHAMPAGNE

FRAISE ROYALE

- Champagne flute
- Blender
- 2 strawberries
- 1–2 tsp. strawberry liqueur
- Champagne for topping up
GARNISH
- 1 strawberry

FRUITY, REFRESHING DRINK

Blend the strawberries and the strawberry liqueur, add them to the champagne flute, and top up with champagne. Garnish with the strawberry.

LIME CHAMPAGNE

- Champagne flute
- 1 ounce lime cordial
- 1 ounce bitter lemon
- Sparkling wine or champagne for topping up
GARNISH
- 1 slice of lime

FRUITY COCKTAIL FOR THE SUMMER

Pour the cordial and bitter lemon into the champagne flute. Top up with the sparkling wine. Perch the slice of lime on the rim of the glass.

FLYING DUTCHMAN

- Highball/Collins glass
- Mixing glass
- 3/4 ounce Pisang Ambon
- 3/4 ounce vodka
- 2 tsp. Malibu or other coconut-flavored liqueur
- 1 dash lime juice
- Sparkling wine or champagne for topping up
GARNISH
- 1 piece of lemon peel
- Slice of lemon or lime
- Sprig of mint

REFRESHING, MEDIUM-DRY DRINK FOR ANY TIME OF THE DAY

Mix all the ingredients together, except the sparkling wine, with ice, in the mixing glass and strain into the highball glass over crushed ice. Top up with sparkling wine and squeeze the lemon peel over the drink. Perch the fruit on the rim of the glass and add the mint to the glass.

Fraise Royale

CHAMPAGNE

PROFESSIONAL

- Highball/Collins glass
- Shaker
- 1 1/2 ounces orange juice
- 1 ounce Campari
- 1 ounce dry vermouth
- 3 1/2 ounces sparkling wine or champagne
  for topping up
GARNISH
- 1 slice of orange

FRUITY, BITTER APERITIF

Shake the orange juice, Campari, and vermouth together, with ice, in the shaker and strain into the glass. Top up with champagne. Perch the slice of orange on the rim of the glass.

MELODY

- Highball/Collins glass
- 3/4 ounce apricot brandy
- 3/4 ounce gin
- 2 tsp. triple sec
- Sparkling wine or champagne for topping up
GARNISH
- 1 slice of orange

FRUITY, LONG DRINK FOR THE EVENING

Mix all the ingredients together, except the sparkling wine, with ice cubes, in the glass. Top up with sparkling wine. Perch the slice of orange on the rim of the glass.

PEPPERMINT FRESH

- Rocks glass
- Shaker
- 1 1/2 ounces peppermint-flavored liqueur
- 2 tsp. lemon juice
- Sparkling wine or champagne for topping up
GARNISH
- Sprig of mint

SPICY, AFTER-DINNER DRINK

Shake the liqueur and lemon juice together, with ice, in the shaker and pour into the glass. Top up with sparkling wine. Hang the sprig of mint over the rim of the glass.

MIRABELL

AROMATIC APERITIF

- Champagne flute
- Shaker
- 3/4 ounce orange-flavored liqueur
- 3/4 ounce gin
- 3/4 ounce sweet red vermouth
- 3/4 ounce orange juice
- Sparkling wine or champagne for topping up

Shake all the ingredients, except the sparkling wine, together, with ice, in the shaker and strain into the glass. Top up with sparkling wine and serve immediately.

FLYING

REFRESHING, TANGY COCKTAIL FOR A PARTY

- Champagne flute
- Shaker
- 3/4 ounce gin
- 3/4 ounce triple sec
- 3/4 ounce lemon juice
- Sparkling wine or champagne for topping up

Shake the gin, triple sec, and lemon juice together, with ice, in the shaker and strain into the glass. Top up with sparkling wine.

FRENCH 76

FRUITY COCKTAIL FOR A PARTY

- Champagne flute
- Shaker
- 1 ounce vodka
- 2 tsp. lemon juice
- 1 tsp. sugar syrup
- Sparkling wine or champagne for topping up

Shake the vodka, lemon juice, and sugar syrup together, with ice, in the shaker and strain into the glass. Top up with sparkling wine.

CHAMPAGNE

MELON SPRITZER

- Cocktail glass
- Blender
- 1 ripe Galia melon
- Grated rind and juice of 1 lemon
- Grated rind and juice of 2 limes
- Sparkling wine or champagne for topping up
- Sugar
GARNISH
- 1 mint sprig

FRUITY, SMOOTH COCKTAIL

Scoop out melon and discard seeds. Place in blender with lemon and lime rinds and juices. Blend until smooth and pour melon purée into glasses. Top up with sparkling wine and garnish with mint. This serves 6–8.

KIWI-FRUIT CHAMPAGNE

- Champagne flute
- Shaker
- 1 1/2 ounces kiwi-fruit flavored liqueur
- 2 tsp. lemon juice
- Sparkling wine or champagne for topping up
GARNISH
- 1 slice of kiwi fruit

FRUITY, SPARKLING COCKTAIL FOR THE EVENING

Shake the kiwi-fruit liqueur and lemon juice together, with ice, in the shaker and strain into the glass. Top up with champagne. Perch the slice of kiwi fruit on the rim of the glass.

VALENCIA

- Champagne flute
- Shaker
- 3/4 ounce apricot brandy
- 3/4 ounce orange juice
- Champagne for topping up
GARNISH
- 1 maraschino cherry

FRUITY CHAMPAGNE APERITIF

Shake all the ingredients, except the champagne, together, with ice, in the shaker and strain into the champagne flute. Top up with champagne. Spear the maraschino cherry on a toothpick and add it to the glass.

Melon Spritzer

CHAMPAGNE

CHAMPENOIS

REFRESHING COCKTAIL FOR A RECEPTION

- Champagne flute
- 1 tsp. apricot brandy
- 1 dash crème de framboise
- 1 dash Angostura bitters
- Champagne for topping up
GARNISH
- 1 slice of orange
- 1 maraschino cherry

Mix all the ingredients together, except the champagne, in the champagne flute. Top up with champagne. Perch the slice of orange on the rim of the glass and fasten the cherry to it with a toothpick.

OVERTURE

AROMATIC APERITIF

- Champagne flute
- 1/2 ounce orange-flavored liqueur
- 1 dash orange bitters
- Dry sparkling wine or champagne for topping up
GARNISH
- 1 orange peel spiral

Pour the liqueur and bitters into the glass, top up with sparkling wine or champagne, and hang the orange peel over the rim of the glass.

SOUTHERN TRIP

TANGY APERITIF

- Champagne flute
- 1 1/2 ounces Southern Comfort
- Dry sparkling wine or champagne for topping up
- 1 piece of orange peel

Pour the Southern Comfort into the champagne flute and top up with sparkling wine or champagne. Squeeze the orange peel over the drink and add the peel to the glass.

CHAMPAGNE SOUR

FRUITY APERITIF

- Champagne flute
- 1 sugar cube
- 1 tbsp. lemon juice
- Sparkling wine or champagne for topping up
GARNISH
- 1 slice of orange

Put the sugar cube into the glass, drizzle the lemon juice over it, and top up with the sparkling wine. Perch the slice of orange on the rim of the glass.

CHICAGO I

FRUITY COCKTAIL FOR A PARTY

- Champagne flute
- Mixing glass
- 3/4 ounce cognac
- 1 tsp. Cointreau
- 1 dash Angostura bitters
- Champagne or sparkling wine for topping up

Mix the cognac, Cointreau, and Angostura bitters together, with ice, in the mixing glass and strain into the champagne flute. Top up with champagne.

CHICAGO II

AROMATIC COCKTAIL FOR THE EVENING

- Champagne glass with sugared rim
- Mixing glass
- 3/4 ounce cognac
- 3 dashes orange curaçao
- 1 dash orange bitters
- Sparkling wine or champagne for topping up

Mix all the ingredients, except the sparkling wine, together, with ice, in the mixing glass and strain into the glass. Top up with sparkling wine.

CHAMPAGNE

COOL GREEN HAZE

- Champagne glass
- Pitcher
- 750 ml. dry sparkling wine or champagne
- 750 ml. lemon-lime soda
- 6 tbsp. melon liqueur
- 6 tbsp. kiwi-fruit flavored liqueur
GARNISH
- 3 kiwi fruits, peeled and chopped
- 1 piece watermelon
- lemon and lime peel twists

EXOTIC FRUITY PUNCH FOR A PARTY

Pour the ingredients into the pitcher with plenty of ice cubes. Decorate with fruit and pour into flute, spooning a little fruit into each glass. Serves 6.

AMARETTO FLIRT

- Champagne glass
- Shaker
- 3/4 ounce amaretto
- 3/4 ounce orange juice
- Dry sparkling wine or champagne for topping up
GARNISH
- 1/2 slice of orange
- 1 maraschino cherry

FRUITY COCKTAIL FOR A RECEPTION

Shake all the ingredients, except the sparkling wine, together, with ice, in the shaker and strain into the cocktail glass. Top up with sparkling wine. Perch the orange on the rim of the glass and fasten the cherry to it with a toothpick.

FRUIT CHAMPAGNE

- Champagne glass
- Shaker
- 1 3/4 ounces orange juice
- 3/4 ounce apricot brandy
- 2 tsp. cognac
- Sparkling wine or champagne for topping up
GARNISH
- 1 maraschino cherry

FRUITY, MILD COCKTAIL FOR THE EVENING

Shake the orange juice, apricot brandy, and cognac together, with ice, in the shaker and strain into the glass. Top up with sparkling wine. Perch the cherry on the rim of the glass.

Cool Green Haze

CHAMPAGNE

ROGER VERGÉ

- Champagne flute
- 1 tsp. crème de cassis
- 1 tsp. orange-flavored liqueur
- Sparkling wine or champagne for topping up
GARNISH
- 1 slice of lemon

FRUITY APERITIF

Pour the crème de cassis and orange liqueur into the glass and top up with sparkling wine. Perch the slice of lemon on the rim of the glass.

JACQUES LAMELOISE

- Champagne flute
- 1 tbsp. plum-flavored liqueur
- 2 tsp. raspberry-flavored liqueur
- Sparkling wine or champagne for topping up
GARNISH
- 1 raspberry

SWEET, MILD COCKTAIL

Pour the liqueurs into the glass and top up with sparkling wine. Perch the raspberry on the rim of the glass.

ROSIE'S

- Highball/Collins glass
- Shaker
- 2³/4 ounces grapefruit juice
- 1¹/2 ounces Campari
- 2 tsp. orange-flavored liqueur
- Sparkling wine or champagne for topping up
GARNISH
- 1 slice of orange

FRUITY, TANGY APERITIF

Shake the grapefruit juice, Campari, and orange-flavored liqueur together, with ice, in the shaker and strain into the glass. Top up with sparkling wine. Perch the slice of orange on the rim of the glass.

SILVER TOP

- Champagne glass
- Shaker
- 3/4 ounce triple sec
- 3/4 ounce gin
- 2 tsp. orange juice
- 1 tsp. grenadine
- Sparkling wine or champagne for topping up
GARNISH
- 1/2 slice of orange
- 2 maraschino cherries

REFRESHING, FRUITY CHAMPAGNE COCKTAIL FOR A PARTY

Shake the triple sec, gin, orange juice, and grenadine together well, with ice, in the shaker and strain into the glass. Top up with champagne. Perch the fruit on the rim of the glass.

AIR MAIL

- Champagne flute
- Shaker
- 1 ounce dark rum
- 3/4 ounce lime cordial
- 2 tsp. honey
- Sparkling wine or champagne for topping up
GARNISH
- 1 slice of lime
- 1 maraschino cherry

SWEET, FRUITY CHAMPAGNE COCKTAIL FOR A PARTY

Shake the rum, lime cordial, and honey together, with ice, in the shaker and pour into the champagne flute. Top up with the champagne. Perch the fruit on the rim of the glass.

SPOTLIGHT

- Champagne glass
- Mixing glass
- 1 ounce cherry-flavored liqueur
- 2 tsp. Campari
- 2 tsp. dry vermouth
- 2 tsp. gin
- Sparkling wine or champagne for topping up
GARNISH
- 1 slice of lemon

FRUITY, SLIGHTLY BITTER APERITIF

Shake all the ingredients, except the sparkling wine, with ice, in the shaker and strain into the glass. Top up with sparkling wine. Perch the slice of lemon on the rim of the glass.

CHAMPAGNE

BLACK VELVET

- Goblet
- 1/4 pint stout
- 1/4 pint champagne or sparkling wine

RICH DRINK FOR THE EVENING

Slowly pour both ingredients, stout first, into glass. Stir gently.

VALENCIA SMILE

- Champagne flute
- Shaker
- 1 ounce apricot brandy
- 3/4 ounce orange juice
- 3 dashes orange bitters
- Sparkling wine or champagne for topping up
GARNISH
- 1 slice of orange

FRUITY COCKTAIL FOR A RECEPTION

Shake all the ingredients together, except the sparkling wine, with ice, in the shaker and strain into the glass. Top up with sparkling wine. Perch the slice of orange on the rim of the glass.

MOONWALK

- Champagne flute
- Shaker
- 1 ounce orange-flavored liqueur
- 1 ounce grapefruit-flavored juice
- 1 dash rose water
- Sparkling wine or champagne for topping up

DELICATELY TANGY CHAMPAGNE COCKTAIL FOR A RECEPTION

Shake the liqueur, grapefruit juice, and rose water together, with ice, in the shaker and strain into the flute. Top up with champagne.

Black Velvet

CHAMPAGNE

FEEL LIKE A HOLIDAY

MILD COCKTAIL FOR A PARTY

- Champagne flute
- Mixing glass
- 2 tsp. vodka
- 2 tsp. raspberry eau-de-vie
- Sparkling wine or champagne for topping up

Mix the vodka and raspberry-eau-de-vie together, with ice, in the mixing glass and strain into the champagne flute. Top up with champagne.

SEXY 6

FRUITY APERITIF

- Champagne glass
- Shaker
- 3/4 ounce gin
- 3/4 ounce orange juice
- 2 tsp. apricot brandy
- 2 tsp. raspberry juice
- Sparkling wine or champagne for topping up
GARNISH
- 1 maraschino cherry

Shake the gin, orange juice, apricot brandy, and raspberry juice together, with ice, in the shaker and strain into the glass. Top up with sparkling wine. Perch the cherry on the rim of the glass.

COLD DUCK

TANGY, FRESH APERITIF

- Champagne glass
- 1 3/4 ounces white wine
- Sparkling wine or champagne for topping up
- Extra: 1 piece of lemon peel

Pour all the ingredients into the glass together. Add the piece of lemon peel to the glass.

BUCKS FIZZ

LIGHT SPARKLING WINE COCKTAIL FOR A RECEPTION OR BRUNCH

- Champagne flute
- Orange juice
- Sparkling wine or champagne for topping up

Half fill the champagne flute with orange juice and top up with sparkling wine.

LONDON FRENCH 75

LIGHT REFRESHING DRINK

- Highball/Collins glass
- Shaker
- 2 ounces gin
- 1/2 ounce lemon juice
- 1/2 tsp. sugar
- Sparkling wine or champagne for topping up

Combine all the ingredients, except the champagne, in a cocktail shaker. Shake well and pour into glass. Top up with champagne.

SOYER AU CHAMPAGNE

SWEET, COOL DRINK

- Wine glass
- 1/4 tsp. cognac
- 1/4 tsp. maraschino liqueur
- 1/4 tsp. triple sec
- 2 tbsp. vanilla ice cream
- Sparkling wine or champagne for topping up
GARNISH
- 1 maraschino cherry

Mix the ice cream with the cognac and liqueurs in the glass. Fill with champagne and stir gently. Garnish with the cherry.

CHAMPAGNE

POINSETTA

- Champagne glass
- 1 tbsp. Grand Marnier or Cointreau
- 1 ounce cranberry juice
- Sparkling wine or champagne for topping up

FRUITY, LIGHT DRINK

Mix the liqueur and cranberry juice in the glass. Top up with champagne.

RED SIN

- Highball/Collins glass
- 1 1/2 ounces crème de cassis
- 2 tsp. orange juice
- Red sparkling wine for topping up
GARNISH
- 1 sprig of redcurrants

FRUITY APERITIF

Mix the crème de cassis and the orange juice in the glass with ice cubes. Top up with red sparkling wine. Hang the sprig of redcurrants over the rim of the glass.

JAMAICA COOLER

- Highball/Collins glass
- 3 1/2 ounces dry red wine
- 1 1/2 ounces light rum
- 1 ounce sugar syrup
- 2 tsp. lemon juice
- 2 tsp. orange juice
GARNISH
- 1/2 slice of lemon

FRUITY COOLER FOR A PARTY

Mix all the ingredients together, with ice cubes, in the glass. Perch the slice of lemon on the rim of the glass. Serve with a straw.

Poinsetta

CHAMPAGNE

RED-WINE FLIP

- Goblet
- Shaker
- 2³/4 ounces red wine
- 1 egg yolk
- 2 tsp. sugar
- Extra: Grated nutmeg

MILD, SPICY DRINK FOR THE EVENING

Shake all the ingredients together, with ice, in the shaker and strain into the goblet. Sprinkle grated nutmeg on top.

SANGRIA

- Highball/Collins glass
- Pitcher
- 2 tbsp. sugar
- Juice of 1 lemon
- Juice of 1 orange
- 1 orange, thinly sliced
- 1 lemon, thinly sliced
- 1 lime, thinly sliced
- 1 bottle of red wine

FRUITY, TANGY DRINK FOR A HOT DAY

Mix ingredients in pitcher, with ice cubes, and stir well. Serve in glass with fruit spooned in.

KIR

- Champagne glass
- ¹/2 ounce crème de cassis
- Dry white wine for topping up

CLASSIC RECEPTION DRINK

Pour liqueur into glass and top up with wine.

SPRITZER

REFRESHING DRINK FOR EVERY DAY

- Large rocks glass
- 4 ounces white wine
- Soda water for topping up
- ¹/2 slice of lemon

Pour the wine into the glass and top up with soda water. Add the slice of lemon to the glass.

SUMMER WINE CUP

FRUITY DRINK FOR A HOT DAY

- Highball/Collins glass
- Punch bowl
- Selection of fresh fruit, such as strawberries, raspberries, grapes, blackcurrants, etc.
- Superfine sugar
- 2 bottles of chilled white wine
- 2 ounces curaçao
- 1 ounce maraschino liqueur

Place fruit in punch bowl. Sprinkle with sugar. Add plenty of ice cubes, then pour in wine, curaçao and maraschino. Chill for one hour. Ladle into glass.

KIR ROYALE

AROMATIC CHAMPAGNE APERITIF

- Champagne flute
- 2 tsp. crème de cassis
- 3¹/2 ounces champagne or dry sparkling wine for topping up

Pour the crème de cassis into the glass and top up with champagne.

TEQUILA, CACHAÇA, AND ANISEED-BASED DRINKS

TEQUILA-CACHAÇA-ANISEED

RIDLEY

SPICY, AFTER-DINNER DRINK

- Rocks glass
- 1 ounce tequila
- 1 ounce gin
- 1 dash Galliano

Half fill the glass with crushed ice. Pour the tequila, gin, and finally the Galliano into the glass. Stir briefly.

LA CONGA

FRUITY, SLIGHTLY BITTER DRINK FOR ANY TIME OF THE YEAR

- Rocks glass
- 1 1/2 ounces tequila
- 2 tsp. pineapple juice
- 2 dashes Angostura bitters
- Soda water for topping up
GARNISH
- 1 slice of lemon

Mix all the ingredients, except the soda water, together, with ice cubes, in the glass. Add soda water to taste and stir briefly. Perch the slice of lemon on the rim of the glass.

TAMPICO

FRUITY, SLIGHTLY TANGY DRINK FOR THE EVENING

- Cocktail glass
- Shaker
- 1 1/2 ounces tequila
- 3/4 ounce papaya juice
- 2 dashes orange bitters
GARNISH
- 1 piece of papaya

Shake the ingredients together, with ice, in the shaker and strain into the glass. Perch the piece of papaya on the rim of the glass.

TEQUILA GIMLET

- Cocktail glass
- Shaker
- 1 1/2 ounces tequila
- 3/4 ounce lemon juice
- 3/4 ounce lime juice

SLIGHTLY SOUR DRINK FOR THE EVENING

Shake all the ingredients together well, with ice cubes, in the shaker and strain into the cocktail glass.

TEQUILA SOUR

- Rocks glass
- Shaker
- 1 ounce lemon juice
- 3/4 ounce tequila
- 3/4 ounce sugar syrup
GARNISH
- 1 maraschino cherry

FRUITY SOUR FOR ANY TIME OF YEAR

Shake all the ingredients together, with ice, in the shaker and strain into the glass. Perch the cherry on the rim of the glass. The drink may be topped up with sparkling water if desired.

MARTINI MAYADOR

- Cocktail glass
- Mixing glass
- 1 1/2 ounces tequila
- 3/4 ounce dry vermouth
GARNISH
- 1 olive

TANGY, SHORT DRINK FOR THE EVENING

Mix the ingredients together, with ice, in the mixing glass and strain into the cocktail glass. Spear the olive on a toothpick and add it to the glass.

TEQUILA SUNRISE

- Highball/Collins glass
- 1 1/2 ounces white tequila
- Orange juice for topping up
- 1/2 slice of orange
- 3/4 ounce grenadine

FRUITY, LONG DRINK FOR HOT DAYS

Pour the tequila and the orange juice together in the highball glass over ice cubes. Float the slice of orange on top of the drink and pour the grenadine on top. Serve with a stirrer.

MEXICAN OLD-FASHIONED

- Rocks glass
- 1 sugar cube
- 1 dash Angostura bitters
- 1 lemon quarter
- 1 orange segment
- 1 maraschino cherry
- 1 3/4 ounces tequila
- Soda water for topping up

BITTERSWEET LONG DRINK FOR A SUMMER PARTY

Put the sugar cube in the glass and soak it in the bitters, then crush it with a spoon. Add the fruit to the glass, pour tequila over the fruit and sugar, and add four ice cubes. Stir well. Top up with soda water and stir again carefully. Serve with a spoon.

TORNADO

- Highball/Collins glass
- Shaker
- 1 1/2 ounces grapefruit juice
- 1 1/2 ounces passion-fruit juice
- 1 ounce tequila
- 3/4 ounce peach-flavored liqueur
- 2 tsp. lime cordial
GARNISH
- 1/2 slice of orange
- 2 maraschino cherries

MEDIUM-DRY DRINK FOR ANY OCCASION

Shake the ingredients together firmly, with ice, in the shaker and strain into the highball glass over crushed ice. Spear the cherries and the slice of orange on a long wooden skewer, so they look like a sail, and put it in the glass. Serve with a stirrer.

Tequila Sunrise

TEQUILA-CACHAÇA-ANISEED

GRACE OF MONACO

AROMATIC, SHORT DRINK FOR THE AFTERNOON

- Cocktail glass
- Mixing glass
- 3/4 ounce white tequila
- 3/4 ounce apricot brandy
- 3/4 ounce mandarin-flavored liqueur
- Extra: 1 piece of lemon peel

Mix the ingredients together, with ice, in the mixing glass and strain into the cocktail glass. Add the piece of lemon peel to the glass.

FROZEN TEQUILA

FRUITY, DELICIOUSLY TANGY DRINK FOR A SUMMER PARTY

- Cocktail glass
- Blender
- 1 1/2 ounces pineapple juice
- 1 ounce tequila
- 2 tsp. lemon juice

Mix all the ingredients together well, with a bar scoop of crushed ice, in the blender and pour into the glass.

FROZEN BLACKBERRY TEQUILA

DRY, FRUITY DRINK FOR A SUMMER PARTY

- Cocktail glass
- Blender
- 1 1/2 ounces tequila
- 3/4 ounce blackberry-flavored liqueur
- 2 tsp. lemon juice
GARNISH
- 1 slice of lemon

Mix all the ingredients together, with a bar scoop full of crushed ice, in the blender and pour into the glass. Perch the slice of lemon on the rim of the glass.

TEQUILA-CACHAÇA-ANISEED

PACIFICO

FRUITY, DELICATELY TANGY DRINK FOR A SUMMER PARTY

- Cocktail glass
- Blender
- 1 1/2 ounces tequila
- 3/4 ounce passion-fruit syrup
- 2 tsp. lemon juice
GARNISH
- 1 slice of lemon

Mix all the ingredients together, with a bar scoop full of crushed ice, in the blender and pour into the glass. Perch the slice of lemon on the rim of the glass.

MEXICAN GUAYABA

FRUITY, ELEGANT, TANGY DRINK FOR A PARTY

- Cocktail glass
- Shaker
- 1 ounce tequila
- 2 tsp. orange juice
- 2 tsp. lime juice
- 2 tsp. guava syrup
- Extra: 1 piece of orange peel

Shake all the ingredients together firmly, with ice, in the shaker and strain into the glass. Squeeze the orange peel over the drink and add the peel to the glass.

TEMPEST

FRUITY, MEDIUM-DRY DRINK FOR ANY OCCASION

- Highball/Collins glass
- Shaker
- 1 ounce tequila
- 2 tsp. mandarin-flavored syrup
- 1 1/2 ounces passion-fruit juice
- 1 1/2 ounces orange juice
- 2 tsp. lemon juice
GARNISH
- 1 slice of star fruit
- 1 maraschino cherry

Shake the ingredients together, with ice, in the shaker and strain into the highball glass, over crushed ice. Perch the slice of star fruit on the rim of the glass and fasten the cherry to the star fruit with a toothpick.

TEQUILA-CACHAÇA-ANISEED

MARGARITA

- Cocktail glass with salted rim
- Shaker
- 2 ounces tequila
- 1½ ounces lime juice
- 1–2 tsp. orange liqueur

POTENT, CLASSIC COCKTAIL

Shake the ingredients together, with ice, in the shaker and pour into the glass.

VIVA

- Highball/Collins glass
- 2 ounces passion-fruit juice
- 2 ounces orange juice
- 1½ ounces white tequila
- ¾ ounce orange curaçao
- 2 tsp. lime juice
GARNISH
- 1 strawberry
- 1 slice of star fruit

FRUITY, LONG DRINK FOR A PARTY

Mix the ingredients together, with ice cubes, in the glass. Spear the slice of star fruit and the strawberry on a toothpick and perch the fruit on the rim of the glass. Serve with a stirrer.

CARABINIERI

- Highball/Collins glass
- Shaker
- 2¾ ounces orange juice
- 1 ounce tequila
- ¾ ounce Galliano
- ¾ ounce lime juice
- 1 egg yolk

FRUITY, DELICATELY TANGY DRINK FOR A SUMMER PARTY

Shake all the ingredients together well, with ice cubes, in the shaker. Half fill the highball glass with crushed ice and strain the drink into the glass.

Margarita

TEQUILA-CACHAÇA-ANISEED

TAPICO

REFRESHING, BITTER DRINK FOR A PARTY

- Highball/Collins glass
- Shaker
- 1½ ounces white tequila
- ¾ ounce crème de cassis
- ¾ ounce banana juice
- Tonic water for topping up
GARNISH
- ½ slice of orange
- 1 maraschino cherry

Shake all the ingredients, except the tonic water, together, with ice, in the shaker and strain into the highball glass over ice cubes. Top up with the tonic water. Spear the slice of orange and the cherry on a toothpick and perch it on the rim of the glass.

ALLELUIA

REFRESHING, FRUITY DRINK FOR A SUMMER PARTY

- Highball/Collins glass
- Shaker
- ¾ ounce white tequila
- ½ ounce maraschino
- ½ ounce blue curaçao
- ½ ounce lemon juice
- 1 dash of egg white
- Bitter lemon for topping up
GARNISH
- 1 slice of lemon
- 2 maraschino cherries
- 1 piece of orange peel
- Sprig of mint

Shake all the ingredients, except the bitter lemon, together, with ice, in the shaker and strain into the highball glass. Top up with the bitter lemon and stir. Spear the slice of lemon and cherries on a toothpick and perch the fruit on the rim of the glass. Add the orange peel and sprig of mint to the glass.

MEXICAN MOCKINGBIRD

SPICY, DELICATELY TANGY DRINK FOR A SUMMER PARTY

- Highball/Collins glass
- Shaker
- 1½ ounces tequila
- ¾ ounce green crème de menthe
- 2 tsp. lime juice
- Soda water for topping up
GARNISH
- Sprig of mint

Shake all the ingredients together, except the soda water, with ice, in the shaker. Fill the highball glass one-third full with ice cubes and strain the drink into the glass. Top up with soda water and stir briefly. Perch the sprig of mint on the rim of the glass.

CHAÇINI

- Cocktail glass
- Mixing glass
- 1 1/2 ounces cachaça
- 2 tsp. light rum
- 2 tsp. dry vermouth
- 1 dash Angostura bitters
- Extra: 1 piece of lemon peel

SPICY, DRY APERITIF

Mix all the ingredients together, with ice, in the mixing glass and strain into the cocktail glass. Squeeze the lemon peel over the drink and add the peel to the glass.

BRASILIA

- Highball/Collins glass
- Shaker
- 1 3/4 ounces orange juice
- 1 3/4 ounces pineapple juice
- 1 1/2 ounces cachaça
- 3/4 ounce cream of coconut
- 2 tsp. blue curaçao
GARNISH
- 1 piece of melon

FRUITY, SWEET DRINK FOR A SUMMER PARTY

Shake all the ingredients together, with ice, in the shaker and strain into the highball glass over crushed ice. Perch the slice of melon on the rim of the glass. Serve with a stirrer.

RECIFE

- Highball/Collins glass
- Shaker
- 2 3/4 ounces pineapple juice
- 1 ounce cachaça
- 3/4 ounce dark rum
- 2 tsp. tequila
- 1 dash orange bitters
GARNISH
- 1/4 slice of pineapple
- 1 maraschino cherry

FRUITY, ELEGANT, TANGY DRINK FOR A SUMMER PARTY

Shake all the ingredients together firmly, with ice, in the shaker and strain into the glass. Top up with crushed ice. Perch the fruit on the rim of the glass.

TEQUILA-CACHAÇA-ANISEED

APRÈS SKI

REFRESHING, SOPHISTICATED DRINK

- Highball/Collins glass
- Shaker
- 1 ounce Pernod
- 1 ounce vodka
- 1 ounce green crème de menthe
- Chilled lemon soda for topping up
GARNISH
- 1 lemon slice
- 1 sprig of mint

Shake all the ingredients, except the lemon soda, together, with ice, in the shaker and strain into the glass. Garnish with the lemon slice and mint.

CARNIVAL

FRUITY, SWEET DRINK FOR A SUMMER PARTY

- Highball/Collins glass
- Shaker
- 2 ounces pineapple juice
- 1 ounce coconut-flavored liqueur
- 1 1/2 ounces cachaça
- 3/4 ounce light cream
- 2 tsp. dark rum
GARNISH
- 1/4 slice of pineapple

Shake all the ingredients together firmly, with ice, in the shaker and strain into the glass. Add a little crushed ice. Perch the slice of pineapple on the rim of the glass.

WALDORF

SPICY APERITIF

- Cocktail glass
- Shaker
- 3/4 ounce Pernod
- 3/4 ounce Irish whiskey
- 2 dashes Angostura bitters

Shake all the ingredients together, with ice, in the shaker and strain into the cocktail glass.

Après Ski

DR. FUNK

MILD, SPICY DRINK FOR THE EVENING

- Highball/Collins glass
- Shaker
- 1 1/2 ounces dark rum
- 3/4 ounce Pernod
- 3/4 ounce lemon juice
- 3/4 ounce lime juice
- 1 ounce grenadine
- Soda water for topping up

Shake all the ingredients, except the soda water, together, with ice, in the shaker and pour into the highball glass. Top up with soda water and stir briefly. Serve with a straw.

DUCHESS

SPICY, ELEGANT, TANGY APERITIF

- Rocks glass
- Mixing glass
- 3/4 ounce pastis
- 3/4 ounce sweet red vermouth
- 3/4 ounce dry vermouth

Mix all the ingredients together well, with ice, in the mixing glass and strain into the glass over ice.

ATOMIC

SPICY, ELEGANT, TANGY DRINK FOR THE EVENING

- Cocktail glass
- Shaker
- 3/4 ounce pastis
- 3/4 ounce brandy
- 1 dash orange bitters

Shake all the ingredients together firmly, with plenty of ice, in the shaker and strain into the glass.

LONDON FOG

- Cocktail glass
- Shaker
- 3/4 ounce anisette
- 3/4 ounce white peppermint-flavored liqueur
- 1 dash Angostura bitters
GARNISH
- Sprig of mint

SPICY DRINK FOR THE EVENING

Shake all the ingredients together, with ice, in the shaker and strain into the glass. Perch the sprig of mint on the rim of the glass.

BLANCHE

- Cocktail glass
- Shaker
- 3/4 ounce anisette
- 3/4 ounce Cointreau
- 3/4 ounce triple sec

ELEGANT, TANGY DRINK FOR THE EVENING

Shake all the ingredients together, with plenty of ice, in the shaker and strain into the glass.

LION'S MILK

- Large rocks glass
- 1 1/2 ounces raki
- Milk for topping up
- Pinch of ground caraway

SPICY, LONG DRINK FOR THE EVENING

Pour the raki into the glass, top up with milk, and stir briefly. Sprinkle a pinch of ground caraway on top.

JELLY BEAN

Tumbler glass
1 ounce blue curaçao
1 ounce grenadine
2 ounces ouzo
Sprite or 7up
GARNISH
Slices of orange and lime

ELEGANT, LONG DRINK FOR THE EVENING

Pour the curaçao, grenadine and ouzo over ice. Stir and top up with Sprite or 7up.

DIXIE

- Cocktail glass
- Shaker
- 3/4 ounce gin
- 2 tsp. Pernod
- 2 tsp. dry vermouth
- 2 tsp. lemon juice
- 2 dashes grenadine

SPICY, FRUITY, TANGY APERITIF

Shake all the ingredients together, with ice, in the shaker and strain into the cocktail glass.

BUNNY HUG

- Cocktail glass
- Shaker
- 3/4 ounce pastis
- 3/4 ounce gin
- 3/4 ounce whiskey

SPICY, ELEGANT, TANGY APERITIF

Shake all the ingredients together, with ice, in the shaker and strain into the cocktail glass.

Jelly Bean

TEQUILA-CACHAÇA-ANISEED

BLOODY JUANITA

PIQUANT, LONG DRINK FOR THE EVENING

- Rocks glass
- 3 1/2 ounces tomato juice
- 1 1/2 ounces tequila
- Ground black pepper
- Celery salt
- Worcestershire sauce
- Hot-pepper sauce

Mix the tomato juice and tequila together, with ice, in the glass. Season to taste with the seasonings.

BOSPHORUS SPRING

SPICY, LONG DRINK FOR HOT DAYS

- Highball/Collins glass
- Shaker
- 3/4 ounce raki
- 3/4 ounce Pernod
- 2 tsp. lemon juice
- 1 tsp. lime cordial
- Soda water for topping up
GARNISH
- 1 lemon peel spiral

Shake all the ingredients together, except the soda water, with crushed ice, in the shaker and strain into the glass. Top up with soda water and stir. Add the lemon peel to the glass.

CLASSIC RAKI

SPICY DRINK FOR THE EVENING

- Small highball/Collins glass
- 1 1/2 ounces raki
- Still mineral water for topping up

Pour the raki into the glass, top up with water, and stir briefly. Add ice to taste.

PERNOD FIZZ

- Highball/Collins glass
- Shaker
- 1 ounce Pernod
- 2 tsp. brandy
- 2 tsp. grenadine
- 3/4 ounce lemon juice
- 3/4 ounce orange juice
- 1 egg white
- Soda water for topping up

SPICY, FRUITY DRINK

Shake all the ingredients, except the soda water, together, with ice, in the shaker and strain into the glass. Top up with soda water and stir briefly.

TELENOVELA

- Highball/Collins glass
- Shaker
- 2 ounces passion-fruit liqueur
- 1 ounce cachaça
- 3/4 ounce coconut-flavored liqueur
- 2 tsp. dark rum
- 2 tsp. cream of coconut
GARNISH
- 1 slice of lime

FRUITY, ELEGANT, TANGY DRINK FOR A SUMMER PARTY

Shake all the ingredients together firmly, with ice, in the shaker and strain into the glass. Add some crushed ice. Perch the slice of lime on the rim of the glass.

GREEN MONKEY

- Rocks glass
- 1 1/2 ounces Galliano
- 2 tsp. Pernod

SPICY, SWEET DRINK FOR A PARTY

First pour the Galliano into the glass, over ice, then pour the Pernod on top and stir.

LIQUEUR AND CALVADOS-BASED DRINKS

LIQUEUR AND CALVADOS

POUSSE-CAFÉ I

SPICY, SWEET AFTER-DINNER DRINK

- Pousse-café glass or tulip-shaped wine glass
- Blue curaçao
- Galliano

Using a measure, pour a little curaçao into the glass. Carefully pour the Galliano over an inverted bar spoon, held inside the glass with the tip touching the wall, so that it floats on top of the layer of curaçao. The layers should not mix.

POUSSE-CAFÉ II

SWEET AFTER-DINNER DRINK

- Pousse-café glass or tulip-shaped wine glass
- Grenadine
- Maraschino
- Blue curaçao

In the above sequence, layer the ingredients in the glass, following the method for Pousse-Café I.

POUSSE-CAFÉ III

SWEET AFTER-DINNER DRINK

- Pousse-café glass or tulip-shaped wine glass
- Maraschino
- Blue curaçao
- Grand Marnier

Layer the ingredients in the glass, following the method for Pousse-Café I.

SUNNY DREAM

- Cocktail glass
- Shaker
- 3/4 ounce apricot brandy
- 1/2 ounce orange juice
- 2 tsp. Cointreau
- 1 scoop vanilla ice cream
GARNISH
- 1/2 slice of orange

SWEET AFTER-DINNER DRINK

Shake all the ingredients together, firmly, without ice, in the shaker and pour into the glass. Perch the slice of orange on the rim of the glass.

SMITH AND WESSON

- Highball/Collins glass
- Shaker
- 4 ounces apricot nectar
- 1 1/2 ounces amaretto
- 3/4 ounce tequila
GARNISH
- Apricot half

FRUITY, SWEET DRINK FOR A PARTY

Shake all the ingredients together, with ice cubes, in the shaker and strain into the highball glass. Add 2 ice cubes. Perch the apricot half on the rim of the glass.

DALLAS

- Highball/Collins glass
- Shaker
- 3/4 ounce crème de banane
- 3/4 ounce blue curaçao
- 3/4 ounce Batida de Coco
- Pineapple juice for topping up
GARNISH
- 1 strawberry
- 1 sprig of mint

CREAMY DRINK FOR A PARTY

Shake all the ingredients, except the pineapple juice, together, with ice, in the shaker and strain into the highball glass over ice. Top up with pineapple juice and stir. Perch the strawberry on the rim of the glass. Add the sprig of mint to the glass. Serve with a stirrer.

LIQUEUR AND CALVADOS

PASSION-FRUIT COOLER

FRUITY, MILD DRINK FOR A PARTY

- Highball/Collins glass
- 4 ounces passion-fruit and white rum spirit
- Rind of 1 lemon, grated
- 2 tsp. sugar
- 6 passion-fruits
- 1 large mango, peeled and chopped
- Juice of 1 lemon
- Juice of 1 lime
- Soda water for topping up
GARNISH
- Lemon and lime slices

Put lemon rind in a saucepan, with 2/3 cup of water. Bring to the boil, stir in sugar and boil for one minute. Remove from heat, cover, and cool. Purée passion-fruit and mango flesh and mix together with lemon and lime juices, and spirit. Put ice cubes in the glass, add the fruit purée and top up with soda water. Add lemon peel to glass. Decorate with lemon and lime slices. Serves 4.

ANGEL'S KISS

SPICY, SWEET DRINK FOR THE AFTERNOON

- Champagne flute
- 1 1/2 ounces brown crème de cacao
- Lightly whipped cream for topping up
GARNISH
- 1 maraschino cherry

Pour the liqueur into the champagne flute. Spoon the cream over the liqueur to form a layer about 3/4 inch thick. Perch the cherry on the rim of the glass.

COCOA CREAM

SPICY, SWEET AFTER-DINNER DRINK

- Cocktail glass
- Shaker
- 1 1/2 ounces brown crème de cacao
- 1 1/2 ounces light cream

Shake the ingredients together, with ice, in the shaker and strain into the glass.

Passion-fruit Cooler

LIQUEUR AND CALVADOS

GOLDEN CADILLAC

- Cocktail glass
- Shaker
- ³/4 ounce white crème de cacao
- ³/4 ounce light cream
- ³/4 ounce Galliano
- ³/4 ounce orange juice

CREAMY, AFTER-DINNER DRINK

Shake the ingredients together, with ice, in the shaker and strain into the glass.

CARIBBEAN CASSIS

- Highball/Collins glass
- Shaker
- 4 ounces orange juice
- 1¹/2 ounces crème de cassis
- ³/4 ounce light rum
- ³/4 ounce lemon juice
GARNISH
- 1 slice of lemon

FRUITY, LONG DRINK FOR A PARTY

Shake all the ingredients together well, with ice, in the shaker, and strain into the glass over ice cubes. Perch the slice of lemon on the rim of the glass.

LAMBADA

- Highball/Collins glass
- Shaker
- ³/4 ounce blue curaçao
- ³/4 ounce Malibu or other coconut-flavored liqueur
- ³/4 ounce peach juice
- 2 tsp. peach-flavored liqueur
- 2 tsp. pineapple juice
GARNISH
- 1 maraschino cherry

FRUITY, LONG DRINK FOR A SUMMER PARTY

Shake the ingredients together, with ice, in the shaker and strain into the highball glass over ice. Perch the cherry on the rim of the glass.

LIQUEUR AND CALVADOS

RED DEVIL

- Cocktail glass
- Shaker
- 3/4 ounce triple sec
- 3/4 ounce Campari
- 3/4 ounce orange juice

LIGHT, BITTER AFTER-DINNER DRINK

Shake the ingredients together, with ice, in the shaker and strain into the glass.

GREAT BRITAIN

- Highball/Collins glass
- Shaker
- 1 1/2 ounces Drambuie
- 3/4 ounce gin
- 1 ounce lemon juice
- Soda water for topping up
GARNISH
- 1 maraschino cherry

FRUITY, TANGY DRINK FOR A PARTY

Shake the Drambuie, gin, and lemon juice together, with ice cubes, in the shaker and strain into the glass. Top up with soda water and stir. Perch the cherry on the rim of the glass.

APRICOT DRAMBUIE

- Highball/Collins glass
- 2 3/4 ounces apricot nectar
- 1 1/2 ounces Drambuie
- 2 tsp. lemon juice
GARNISH
- 1 slice of lemon

FRUITY, MILD DRINK FOR A PARTY

Mix the ingredients together, with ice cubes, in the highball glass. Perch the slice of lemon on the rim of the glass.

LIQUEUR AND CALVADOS

SASSY

- Rocks glass
- Mixing glass
- 1/2 ounce Drambuie
- 2 tbsp. orange juice
- 2 tbsp. lemon juice
- Tonic water for topping up
GARNISH
- Orange and lemon slices

FRUITY, REFRESHING COCKTAIL

Mix the Drambuie, lemon and orange juice in the mixing glass with ice cubes. Strain this into the rocks glass, add some ice cubes, and top up with tonic water. Garnish with fruit slices.

GALLIANO SOUR

- Rocks glass
- Shaker
- 3/4 ounce Galliano
- 3/4 ounce scotch
- 3/4 ounce lemon juice
- 2 tsp. sugar syrup

FRUITY, SPICY DRINK FOR ANY TIME OF YEAR

Shake all the ingredients together, with ice, in the shaker and strain into the chilled glass.

GREEN CAT

- Cocktail glass
- Shaker
- 1 1/2 ounces kiwi-fruit flavored liqueur
- 3/4 ounce light rum
- 2 dashes lemon juice
- 1 dash Frothee
GARNISH
- 1 maraschino cherry

SOUR SHORT DRINK FOR A PARTY

Shake all the ingredients together, with ice, in the shaker and strain into the cocktail glass. Spear the cherry on a toothpick and add it to the glass.

Sassy

LIQUEUR AND CALVADOS

BODIL

- Cocktail glass
- Shaker
- 3/4 ounce Parfait Amour
- 3/4 ounce green crème de menthe
- 2 tsp. cocoa-flavored liqueur
- 2 tsp. light cream
- Extra: Grated nutmeg

CREAMY, SWEET DRINK FOR THE AFTERNOON

Shake the ingredients together, with ice, in the shaker and strain into the glass. Sprinkle a little nutmeg on top.

DREAM OF LOVE

- Highball/Collins glass
- Shaker
- 2 3/4 ounces pineapple juice
- 1 ounce peach-flavored liqueur
- 3/4 ounce Malibu or other coconut-flavored liqueur
- 2 tsp. blue curaçao
- 2 tsp. lemon juice
GARNISH
- 1 small slice of melon
- 1 maraschino cherry
- 1 orchid

FRUITY, LONG DRINK FOR A PARTY

Shake the ingredients together, with ice, in the shaker and strain into the highball glass over crushed ice or ice cubes. Perch the slice of melon and maraschino cherry on the rim of the glass with the orchid.

JUNGLE JUICE

- Highball/Collins glass
- Shaker
- 1 3/4 ounces orange juice
- 3/4 ounce Pisang Ambon
- 3/4 ounce lemon juice
- 2 tsp. apricot brandy
- 2 tsp. gin
GARNISH
- 1 piece of pineapple
- 1 maraschino cherry

FRUITY, SWEET DRINK FOR A PARTY

Shake all the ingredients together, with ice, in the shaker and strain into the highball glass over crushed ice. Perch the piece of pineapple on the rim of the glass and fasten the maraschino cherry to it with a small toothpick.

PINK SOUTHERN COMFORT

SPICY, MILD DRINK FOR A PARTY

- Rocks glass
- Shaker
- 3/4 ounce Southern Comfort
- 3/4 ounce light rum
- 2 tsp. grapefruit juice
- 2 dashes grenadine

Shake all the ingredients together, with ice cubes, in the shaker and strain into the rocks glass over ice cubes.

SOUTHERN SUMMER

FRUITY, MILD DRINK FOR A SUMMER PARTY

- Highball/Collins glass
- Shaker
- 1 1/2 ounces Southern Comfort
- 1 1/2 ounces Canadian whiskey
- 2 tsp. lemon juice
- Ginger ale for topping up
GARNISH
- 1 slice of lemon
- 1 maraschino cherry

Shake all the ingredients, except the ginger ale, together, with ices cubes, in the shaker and strain into the highball glass over ice cubes. Top up with ginger ale and stir briefly. Perch the slice of lemon on the rim of the glass and fasten the cherry to it with a toothpick.

SOUTHERN COLA

SWEET, LONG DRINK FOR THE EVENING

- Highball/Collins glass
- 1 1/2 ounces Southern Comfort
- Cola for topping up
GARNISH
- 1 slice of lemon

Pour the Southern Comfort into the highball glass over ice cubes. Top up with cola and stir briefly. Perch the slice of lemon on the rim of the glass. Serve with a straw.

LIQUEUR AND CALVADOS

VELVET GLOVE

SWEET, CREAMY DRINK FOR A PARTY

- Brandy glass with coffee-rim
- Shaker
- 1 ounce coffee-flavored liqueur
- 1/2 ounce amaretto
- 1 ounce cream
- Extra: chopped chocolate, finely grated

Shake all the ingredients, with ice, in the shaker and strain into glass. Top with finely grated chopped chocolate.

V.W.

AROMATIC, PEAR-FLAVORED APERITIF

- Cocktail glass
- Mixing glass
- 1 ounce Poire William
- 1 ounce sweet white vermouth
GARNISH
- 1 maraschino cherry

Mix the ingredients, with ice, in the mixing glass and strain into the cocktail glass. Spear the cherry on a toothpick and add it to the glass.

VELVET HAMMER

SWEET AFTER-DINNER DRINK

- Cocktail glass
- Shaker
- 3/4 ounce Tia Maria or other coffee-flavored liqueur
- 3/4 ounce Cointreau
- 3/4 ounce light cream

Shake the ingredients together, with ice, in the shaker and strain into the cocktail glass.

Velvet Glove

LIQUEUR AND CALVADOS

APPLEJACK RABBIT

FRUITY, DELICATELY TANGY DRINK FOR THE EVENING

- Cocktail glass
- Shaker
- 3/4 ounce Calvados
- 3/4 ounce orange juice
- 3/4 ounce lemon juice
- 3/4 ounce maple syrup
GARNISH
- 1/2 slice of orange

Shake all the ingredients together firmly, with ice, in the shaker and strain into the glass. Perch the slice of orange on the rim of the glass.

APPLE BLOSSOM

FRUITY, DELICATELY TANGY DRINK FOR A SUMMER PARTY

- Champagne glass
- Blender
- 1 ounce Calvados
- 3/4 ounce apple juice
- 1 tbsp. maple syrup
- 2 tsp. lemon juice
GARNISH
- 1 slice of lemon

Mix all the ingredients together briefly, with a scoop of crushed ice, in the blender and pour into the champagne glass. Perch the slice of lemon on the rim.

NEW YORKER APPLE

FRUITY, DELICATELY TANGY APERITIF

- Cocktail glass
- Mixing glass
- 1 1/2 ounces Calvados
- 3/4 ounce sweet red vermouth
- 1 dash orange bitters
GARNISH
- 1 maraschino cherry

Mix all the ingredients together, with ice, in the mixing glass and strain into the glass. Perch the cherry on the rim of the glass.

KICKER

- Cocktail glass
- Mixing glass
- 3/4 ounce Calvados
- 3/4 ounce dark rum
- 3/4 ounce sweet red vermouth

GARNISH
- I maraschino cherry

SPICY, RATHER SWEET AFTER-DINNER DRINK

Mix all the ingredients together, with ice, in the mixing glass and strain into the cocktail glass. Add the cherry to the glass.

JACK COLLINS

- Highball/Collins glass
- I 1/2 ounces Calvados
- 3/4 ounce lemon juice
- 2 tsp. sugar syrup
- Soda water for topping up

GARNISH
- 1/2 slice of lemon
- I maraschino cherry

REFRESHING COLLINS FOR ANY TIME OF THE DAY

Mix all the ingredients, except the soda water, together, with ice, in the glass. Top up with soda water and stir well. Perch the slice of lemon on the rim of the glass and add the cherry to the glass. Serve with a long stirrer.

MOONLIGHT CUP

- Highball/Collins glass
- Shaker
- 2 ounces apple juice
- I 1/2 ounces Calvados
- 1/2 tsp. sugar
- Ginger ale for topping up

GARNISH
- I slice of lemon

MILD, FRUITY DRINK FOR THE EVENING

Shake all the ingredients, except the ginger ale, together, with ice, in the shaker and strain into the glass. Top up with ginger ale and stir briefly. Add the slice of lemon to the glass.

FORTIFIED WINE, BITTERS, AND EAUX-DE-VIE-BASED DRINKS

FORTIFIED WINE AND BITTERS

FIVE O'CLOCK

SPICY DRINK FOR THE EVENING

- Cocktail glass
- Shaker
- 3/4 ounce sweet red vermouth
- 3/4 ounce gin
- 3/4 ounce light rum
- 3/4 ounce orange juice

Shake all the ingredients together firmly, with ice cubes, in the shaker and strain into the glass.

CHORUS GIRL

FRUITY, ELEGANT, TANGY DRINK FOR A PARTY

- Cocktail glass
- Shaker
- 3/4 ounce sweet red vermouth
- 3/4 ounce dry vermouth
- 3/4 ounce gin
- 3/4 ounce orange juice
GARNISH
- 1 maraschino cherry

Shake all the ingredients together firmly, with ice, in the shaker and strain into the glass. Perch the cherry on the rim of the glass.

FLORA McDONALD

SPICY, ELEGANT, TANGY DRINK FOR THE EVENING

- Cocktail glass
- Shaker
- 1 1/2 ounces dry vermouth
- 3/4 ounce Drambuie
- 3/4 ounce gin
GARNISH
- 1 slice of orange

Shake all the ingredients together firmly, with ice, in the shaker and strain into the glass. Perch the slice of orange on the rim of the glass.

FORTIFIED WINE AND BITTERS

MERMAID

- Highball/Collins glass
- 3/4 ounce sweet white vermouth
- 3/4 ounce gin
- 3/4 ounce blue curaçao
- Bitter orange for topping up
GARNISH
- 1 lemon peel spiral
- 1 slice of orange

FRUITY, DELICATELY TANGY DRINK FOR A SUMMER PARTY

Mix all the ingredients, except the bitter orange, together, with ice cubes, in the glass. Top up with bitter orange and stir briefly. Hang the spiral of peel over the rim of the glass and perch the slice of orange on the rim also.

TEXAS RANCHER

- Rocks glass
- Shaker
- 1 1/2 ounces grapefruit juice
- 1 ounce dry vermouth
- 3/4 ounce sweet white vermouth
- 3/4 ounce gin
- 1 tsp. maraschino
GARNISH
- 1/4 slice of grapefruit

SPICY, ELEGANT, TANGY DRINK FOR ANY TIME OF YEAR

Shake all the ingredients together, with ice, in the shaker and strain into the glass. Perch the slice of grapefruit on the rim of the glass.

GOLD LION

- Highball/Collins glass
- 4 ounces orange juice
- 1 1/2 ounces sweet red vermouth
- 3/4 ounce vodka
- 3/4 ounce lemon juice
GARNISH
- 1 slice of orange
- Sprig of mint

FRUITY, ELEGANT, TANGY DRINK FOR THE EVENING

Mix all the ingredients together well, with ice cubes, in the highball glass. Perch the slice of orange and sprig of mint on the rim of the glass. Serve with a stirrer and straw.

FORTIFIED WINE AND BITTERS

AMERICANO

TANGY, FRUITY EVENING DRINK

- Rocks glass
- I ounce Campari
- I ounce sweet red vermouth
- Soda water for topping up
GARNISH
- Orange slice
- Lime slice
- I maraschino cherry

Fill the glass with the Campari and vermouth and some ice cubes. Fill up with soda water. Fix the orange and lime slice on a toothpick, with the cherry in the center and perch on the rim of the glass.

BETSY ROSS

FRUITY, ELEGANT, TANGY APERITIF

- Cocktail glass
- Shaker
- I ounce port
- I ounce cognac
- I dash orange-flavored liqueur
- I dash Angostura bitters
- Extra: I piece of lemon peel

Shake all the ingredients together, with ice, and strain into the glass. Squeeze the lemon peel over the drink.

TAYLOR-MADE

FRUITY DRINK FOR HOT DAYS

- Cobbler glass
- 1 3/4 ounces port
- 3/4 ounce B&B liqueur
- 2 dashes orange bitters
- Extra: 2 peach quarters, 2 halved strawberries, and 4 balls of honeydew melon

Fill the glass half full with crushed ice and mix the ingredients together in the glass. Add the fruit to the glass.

Americano

FORTIFIED WINE AND BITTERS

INCA

- Cocktail glass
- Mixing glass
- 3/4 ounce medium sherry
- 3/4 ounce dry vermouth
- 3/4 ounce sweet red vermouth
- 3/4 ounce gin
- 1 dash orange bitters
- Extra: 1 piece of lemon peel

SPICY, ELEGANT, TANGY APERITIF

Mix all the ingredients together, with ice, in the mixing glass and strain into the glass. Squeeze the lemon peel over the drink.

APPETIZER

- Champagne or cocktail glass
- Shaker
- 3/4 ounce Dubonnet
- 3/4 ounce gin
- 3/4 ounce orange juice
- 3 dashes Angostura bitters

TANGY APERITIF

Shake all the ingredients together, with ice, in the shaker and strain into the glass.

DRUGSTORE

- Cocktail glass
- 1 ounce herbal bitters
- 3/4 ounce sweet red vermouth
- 2 tsp. white crème de menthe

BITTER AFTER-DINNER DRINK

Mix the ingredients together in the glass.

FORTIFIED WINE AND BITTERS

CYNAR AND ORANGE

- Highball/Collins glass
- 1 1/2 ounces Cynar
- 1 dash orange bitters
- Orange juice for topping up
GARNISH
- 1 slice of orange

ELEGANT, TANGY APERITIF

Mix the Cynar and orange bitters together, with ice cubes, in the highball glass. Top up with the orange juice and stir briefly. Perch the slice of orange on the rim of the glass.

SIENA

- Cocktail glass
- Mixing glass
- 3/4 ounce Aperol
- 3/4 ounce gin
- 3/4 ounce sweet white vermouth
GARNISH
- 1 maraschino cherry

SPICY, REFINED, TANGY DRINK FOR THE EVENING

Mix all the ingredients together, with ice, in the mixing glass and strain into the glass. Perch the cherry on the rim of the glass.

NATALIA

- Cocktail glass
- Mixing glass
- 3/4 ounce Amaro Siciliano
- 3/4 ounce gin
- 3/4 ounce sweet white vermouth
- 1 dash orange-flavored liqueur
GARNISH
- 1/2 slice of orange

SPICY, ELEGANT, TANGY AFTER-DINNER DRINK

Mix all the ingredients together, with ice, in the mixing glass and strain into the cocktail glass. Perch the slice of orange on the rim of the glass.

FORTIFIED WINE AND BITTERS

FUZZY NAVEL

FRUITY, REFRESHING DRINK

- Highball/Collins glass
- Shaker
- 2 ounces vodka
- 1 ounce peach schnapps
- 8 ounces orange juice
GARNISH
- 1 orange slice

Combine all the ingredients, with ice, in a shaker. Shake well and pour into the glass. Garnish with the orange slice.

PINKY

MEDIUM-DRY, CREAMY DRINK FOR A PARTY

- Highball/Collins glass
- Shaker
- 2 ounces pineapple juice
- 1 1/2 ounces cream of coconut
- 1 ounce Aperol
- 3/4 ounce gin
GARNISH
- 1 piece of pineapple
- 1 maraschino cherry
- 1 sprig of mint

Shake the ingredients together firmly, with ice, in the shaker and strain into the glass. Spear the piece of pineapple, the cherry, and the sprig of mint on a toothpick, and perch on the rim of the glass.

APRICAMP

TANGY, FRUITY DRINK FOR A PARTY

- Goblet or red wine glass
- Mixing glass
- 1 ounce Campari
- 1 ounce apricot brandy
- Orange juice for topping up
- Extra: 1 piece of orange peel

Mix the Campari and apricot brandy together, with ice, in the mixing glass and strain into the glass. Top up with orange juice and stir again. Add the orange peel to the glass.

Fuzzy Navel

FORTIFIED WINE AND BITTERS

NORTHERN LIGHTS

SPICY, ELEGANT, TANGY DRINK FOR A SUMMER PARTY

- Rocks glass
- Shaker
- 3/4 ounce aquavit
- 3/4 ounce Canadian whiskey
- 1 tsp. grenadine
- 1 dash Angostura bitters
- Soda water for topping up
- Extra: 1 lemon wedge and 1 orange segment

Shake all the ingredients, except the soda water, together, with ice, in the shaker and strain into the glass over ice cubes. Add the fruit to the glass, top up with soda water, and stir briefly.

KIRSCH COCKTAIL

STRONG, SHORT DRINK FOR THE EVENING

- Cocktail glass
- Mixing glass
- 1 3/4 ounces kirsch
- 2 tsp. grenadine
- 1 dash triple sec
GARNISH
- 1 maraschino cherry

Mix all the ingredients together, with ice, in the mixing glass and strain into the cocktail glass. Spear the cherry on a toothpick and lay the garnish across the rim of the glass.

HELVETIA

SWEET, AFTER-DINNER DRINK

- Cocktail glass
- Shaker
- 3/4 ounce kirsch
- 3/4 ounce cherry brandy
- 3/4 ounce light cream
- 2 tsp. grenadine
GARNISH
- 1 maraschino cherry

Shake all the ingredients together firmly, with ice, in the shaker and strain into the glass. Then spear the cherry on a toothpick and lay the garnish across the rim of the glass.

FORTIFIED WINE AND BITTERS

GRAPPON

- Cocktail glass
- Shaker
- 1 1/2 ounces grappa
- 3/4 ounce peach brandy
- 3/4 ounce lemon juice
- Extra: 1 piece of lemon peel

FRUITY, ELEGANT, TANGY DRINK FOR THE EVENING

Shake all the ingredients together, with ice, in the shaker and strain into the glass. Squeeze the lemon peel over the drink and add it to the glass.

KORN KIR

- Rocks glass
- Mixing glass
- 3/4 ounce korn schnapps
- 3/4 ounce crème de cassis
- 3/4 ounce black-currant juice
- Soda water for topping up

MILD, FRUITY DRINK FOR THE EVENING

Shake all the ingredients, except the soda water, together, with ice cubes, in the shaker and strain into the glass. Top up with soda water.

SWEET WILLIAM

- Cocktail glass
- Shaker
- 3/4 ounce Poire William
- 3/4 ounce apricot brandy
- 3/4 ounce light cream
GARNISH
- 1 maraschino cherry

MILD, FRUITY AFTER-DINNER DRINK

Shake all the ingredients together firmly, with ice, in the shaker and strain into the glass. Perch the cherry on the rim of the glass.

NON-ALCOHOLIC
DRINKS

NON-ALCOHOLIC

BLACK FOREST FLIP

FRUITY, TANGY DRINK FOR ANY TIME OF YEAR

- Tulip-shaped glass
- Shaker
- 2 ounces cherry juice
- 3/4 ounce lime cordial
- 2 tsp. lemon juice
- 1 egg yolk
GARNISH
- 1 small sprig lemon balm

Shake all the ingredients together, with ice cubes, in the shaker and strain into the glass.

CABRIOLET 911

REFRESHING, RATHER BITTER DRINK FOR THE EVENING

- Highball/Collins glass
- Shaker
- 3/4 ounce non-alcoholic blue curaçao
- 3/4 ounce grapefruit juice
- 2 tsp. lime cordial
- Tonic water for topping up
GARNISH
- 1 small cluster grapes

Shake all the ingredients, except the tonic water, together, with ice, in the shaker. Strain into the highball glass and top up with tonic water. Hang the cluster of grapes over the rim of the glass. Serve with a stirrer.

LEMON COOLER

TANGY COOLER FOR THE SUMMER

- Highball/Collins glass
- Shaker
- 1 1/2 ounces lemon juice
- 3/4 ounce lime syrup
- 3/4 ounce lime juice
- Bitter lemon for topping up
GARNISH
- 1 slice of lemon
- 2 maraschino cherries

Shake all the ingredients, except the bitter lemon, together, with ice, in the shaker. Strain into the highball glass over the ice and top up with bitter lemon. Perch the slice of lemon on the rim of the glass. Fasten one cherry to it with a toothpick. Put the other cherry in the glass. Serve with a stirrer.

FLORIDA COCKTAIL

FRUITY, SWEET DRINK FOR ANY OCCASION

- Large cocktail glass
- Shaker
- 2 ounces pineapple juice
- 1 ounce lemon juice
- 2 tsp. non-alcoholic grenadine
- 1 dash Angostura bitters

Shake all the ingredients together well, with ice cubes, in the shaker, and strain into the glass.

PLANTER'S WONDER

FRUITY, SWEET DRINK FOR A PARTY

- Highball/Collins glass
- Shaker
- 2 ounces orange juice
- 2 ounces pineapple juice
- 2 ounces passion-fruit juice
- 3/4 ounce lemon juice
- 3/4 ounce non-alcoholic grenadine

GARNISH
- 1 slice of star fruit
- 1 slice of kiwi fruit
- 1 maraschino cherry

Shake all the ingredients together well, with ice cubes, in the shaker and strain into the highball glass over the crushed ice. Spear the pieces of fruit on a toothpick and lay the garnish across the rim of the glass.

ARGENTINA

FRUITY, SWEET DRINK FOR A PARTY

- Large highball/Collins glass
- Shaker
- 1 3/4 ounces pineapple juice
- 1 3/4 ounces apricot juice
- 1 3/4 ounces passion-fruit juice
- 1 3/4 ounces papaya juice
- 3/4 ounce lemon juice
- 3/4 ounce non-alcoholic grenadine

GARNISH
- 1/4 slice of pineapple
- 1 maraschino cherry

Shake the juices and grenadine together, with ice, in the shaker and strain into the highball glass over crushed ice. Spear the slice of pineapple and the cherry on a toothpick and lay the garnish across the rim of the glass.

NON-ALCOHOLIC

ORANGE AND PINEAPPLE CRUSH

FRUITY, REFRESHING DRINK

- Large highball/Collins glass
- Blender
- 1 pineapple
- 3 ounces orange juice
- 2 tbsp. lemon juice
- Soda water for topping up
GARNISH
- Chunks of pineapple
- Orange slices

Combine the ingredients in the blender. Pour over ice cubes into the glass. Top up with soda water and stir gently. Garnish with fruit. Serve with a straw.

FRUIT CUP

FRUITY, TANGY DRINK FOR A PARTY

- Highball/Collins glass
- Shaker
- 2³/4 ounces orange juice
- 2 ounces pineapple juice
- 2 ounces lime juice
- ³/4 ounce lemon juice
- ³/4 ounce non-alcoholic grenadine
GARNISH
- 1 slice of orange
- ¹/2 slice of lemon
- 3 maraschino cherries
- 1 pineapple segment

Shake all the ingredients together, with plenty of ice, in the shaker and strain into the highball glass. Perch the slice of orange on the rim of the glass and add the remaining fruit to the glass.

STEFFI GRAF

FRUITY, SWEET DRINK

- Highball/Collins glass
- Mixing glass
- 1¹/2 ounces pear juice
- 1¹/2 ounces apricot juice
- 1¹/2 ounces kiwi-fruit juice
- 1¹/2 ounces orange juice
GARNISH
- 1 slice of kiwi fruit
- 1 slice of orange
- 1 mini pear, peeled

Mix all the ingredients together, with ice cubes, in the mixing glass and strain into the highball glass. Spear the fruit on a toothpick and lay the garnish across the rim of the glass.

Orange and Pineapple Crush

NON-ALCOHOLIC

BABOUIN

- Highball/Collins glass
- Shaker
- 1 3/4 ounces cherry juice
- 1 1/2 ounces passion-fruit juice
- 1 ounce pineapple juice
- 3/4 ounce lime juice
- 2 tsp. orange juice
- Extra: 1/4 banana, peeled and sliced, pieces of pineapple, and 2 maraschino cherries.

FRUITY, LONG DRINK FOR A PARTY

Shake all the ingredients together, with ice cubes, in the shaker and strain into the highball glass. Put the pieces of fruit in the glass. Serve with a spoon or long toothpick.

ANASTASIA

- Large brandy snifter
- Shaker
- 2 slices of pineapple, diced
- 2 ounces pineapple juice
- 1 1/2 ounces orange juice
- 1 ounce apple juice
- 3/4 ounce lemon juice
- Ginger ale for topping up
GARNISH
- 1 maraschino cherry

FRUITY, MILD DRINK FOR A PARTY

Put the diced pineapple into the brandy snifter. Shake the juices together, with ice cubes, in the shaker and strain into the glass over the pineapple. Top up with ginger ale and stir briefly. Spear the cherry on a toothpick and lay the garnish across the rim of the glass.

PINCASSO

- Highball/Collins glass
- Shaker
- 1 3/4 ounces red grape juice
- 1 1/2 ounces grapefruit juice
- 3/4 ounce lime juice
- 2 tsp. non-alcoholic grenadine
- 2 tsp. bitter lemon
- Soda water for topping up
GARNISH
- 1 sprig of lemon balm

FRUITY, TANGY DRINK FOR A PARTY

Shake the juices and grenadine together, with ice cubes, in the shaker and strain into the highball glass. Add the bitter lemon, top up with soda water, and stir. Perch the sprig of lemon balm on the rim of the glass.

BITTER CHERRIES

- Highball/Collins glass
- 1 1/2 ounces orange juice
- 1 1/2 ounces cherry nectar
- 3 1/2 ounces Sanbitter

GARNISH
- 1 slice of orange

FRUITY, BITTER APERITIF

Mix the juice and nectar together, with ice cubes, in the highball glass. Top up with Sanbitter and stir briefly. Perch the slice of orange on the rim of the glass.

PALERMO

- Highball/Collins glass
- 1 1/2 ounces orange juice
- 1 1/2 non-alcoholic vermouth
- 2 tsp. non-alcoholic grenadine
- 3 1/2 ounces Sanbitter or other non-alcoholic bitters

GARNISH
- 1 slice of orange

SPICY, TANGY DRINK FOR HOT DAYS

Mix the orange juice, vermouth, and grenadine together, with ice cubes, in the highball glass. Top up with the Sanbitter and stir briefly. Perch the slice of orange on the rim of the glass.

WOODRUFF SHAKE

- Highball/Collins glass
- Blender
- 1 scoop lemon sorbet
- 5 tbsp. buttermilk
- 1 tbsp. woodruff syrup
- 1/4 sourish apple, peeled and diced
- 2 tsp. lime juice
- 1 tsp. light cream

GARNISH
- 1 sprig lemon balm

FRUITY, SOURISH DRINK WITH BUTTERMILK FOR THE SUMMER

Put the sorbet in the highball glass. Mix the remaining ingredients together in the blender and pour into the glass. Perch the sprig of lemon balm on the rim of the glass.

NON-ALCOHOLIC

VEGETABLE COCKTAIL

SPICY, PIQUANT DRINK WITH BUTTERMILK FOR EVERY DAY

- Large cocktail glass
- Blender
- 1 ounce carrot juice
- 1 ounce celery juice
- 1 tsp. lemon juice
- 1 tsp. honey
- 3 1/2 ounces buttermilk
- Herb-flavored salt or salt and mixed herbs
- Ground white pepper
GARNISH
- A few celery leaves

Mix all the ingredients together well in the blender and pour into the glass. Float the celery leaves on the drink.

TOMATO PICANTE

SPICY, PIQUANT DRINK

- Large champagne glass
- Blender
- 3 1/2 ounces tomato juice
- 1 tsp. lemon juice
- 1 3/4 ounces buttermilk
- 1-2 tbsp. Sangrita picante
- Ground white pepper
- Salt
GARNISH
- 1 tbsp. sour cream
- 1 tsp. snipped fresh chives

Mix all the ingredients together well in the blender and pour into the champagne glass. Stir the sour cream and chives together and garnish the drink with a spoonful of the mixture.

PRAIRIE OYSTER

SPICY, PIQUANT PICK-ME-UP

- Cocktail glass
- Mixing glass
- 5 dashes Worcestershire sauce
- 1 tsp. olive oil
- 2 dashes hot-pepper sauce
- Freshly ground black pepper and salt
- 2 tbsp. tomato catsup
- 1 egg yolk
- Sweet paprika

Put the Worcestershire sauce, then the oil, hot-pepper sauce, salt, pepper, and catsup into the glass. Put the whole egg yolk in the middle of the liquid and season with paprika. Do not stir!

POWER JUICE

- Rocks glass
- Mixing glass
- 3 1/2 ounces beet juice
- 3 1/2 ounces carrot juice
- 3/4 ounce lemon juice
- Freshly ground black pepper
GARNISH
- 1 long, thin piece of cucumber

SPICY, PIQUANT DRINK FOR MORNINGS AND AFTERNOONS

Mix the juices together in the mixing glass, season to taste with a little pepper, and pour into the glass over ice cubes. Perch the piece of cucumber on the rim of the glass.

JOGGER'S DRINK

- Highball/Collins glass
- Blender
- 4 1/2 ounces vegetable juice
- 3 1/2 ounces buttermilk
- Pinch grated fresh horseradish
- 1 dash lemon juice
- Ground white pepper
- Salt
GARNISH
- 1 tsp. snipped fresh chives

SPICY, PIQUANT DRINK WITH BUTTERMILK FOR EVERY DAY

Mix all the ingredients together well in the blender and pour into the highball glass. Sprinkle the snipped chives on top.

DRYAD

- Champagne glass
- Blender
- 2 1/2 ounces mixed fresh fruits, such as raspberries, blackberries, and blueberries
- 1 tbsp. unsweetened elderberry juice
- 2 tsp. raspberry syrup
- 5 tbsp. plain yogurt
GARNISH
- 1 tbsp. whipped cream

FRUITY, SOUR DRINK WITH YOGURT FOR THE SUMMER

Reserve a few blackberries. Mix all the ingredients together in the blender and pour into the champagne glass. Garnish with a rosette of cream and the reserved blackberries.

INDEX

INDEX

INDEX